The Incredible
MR. DON KNOTTS

The Incredible

MR. DON KNOTTS

An
Eye-Popping
Look at His
Movies

STEPHEN COX
KEVIN MARHANKA

CUMBERLAND HOUSE
NASHVILLE, TENNESSEE

THE INCREDIBLE MR. DON KNOTTS
PUBLISHED BY CUMBERLAND HOUSE PUBLISHING
431 Harding Industrial Drive
Nashville, Tennessee 37211

Cover design: Gore Studio, Inc.
Text design: Mary Sanford

Library of Congress Cataloging-in-Publication Data
Cox, Stephen, 1966–
   The incredible Mr. Don Knotts : an eye-popping look at his movies / Stephen Cox and Kevin Marhanka.
      p. cm.
   Includes index.
   ISBN-13: 978-1-58182-658-6 (hardcover)
   ISBN-10: 1-58182-658-3 (hardcover)
   1. Knotts, Don, 1924–2006. I. Marhanka, Kevin, 1969– II. Title.
   PN2287.K675C69 2008
   791.45'028'092—dc22
   [B]

                                                    2008035710

Printed in the United States of America
1 2 3 4 5 6 7—14 13 12 11 10 09 08

For Don Knotts . . . thanks for all the laughter.
And for my sister Bernadette, who loves fun movies too.

STEPHEN COX

* * *

For my parents, Albert and Ingrid Marhanka, who continue to show
endless love and support throughout my life.

Also for my daughters, Kirstan and Kaitlin, who have shared the
love and laughter of Don Knotts films with me.

KEVIN MARHANKA

Contents

✳ The Movies ✳

"When you work with words, words are your work."

—LUTHER HEGGS,
THE GHOST AND MR. CHICKEN

Acknowledgments

The authors are forever thankful to Don Knotts for granting interviews over a period of a decade while this book took form. This would not have been possible without the unselfish, unbridled enthusiasm of the following people—all fellow fans of Don Knotts—who assisted in a variety of ways during preparation of this tribute to the comedian. Some knew Don, others worked with him, all loved him. Words may fail us here, but please know, by all means, we are grateful. With immense thanks to: Maureen Arthur, Ed Asner, Scott Awley, Ken Beck, Randy Bish, Bart Boatwright, Phil Bowling, Brad and Susan Buescher, Craig Caito, Al Checco, Jim Clark, Steven Colbert, Carole Cook, Tim Conway, Jerry and Blanche Cox, Brian Cox, Dave and Bernadette Dalton, Megan Dalton, Joyce DeWitt, Mark Evanier, Joan Freeman, Sandra Gould, Everett Greenbaum, Andy Griffith, Tom Hill, Al Hirschfeld, Skip Homier, Ron Howard, Justin Humphreys, Larry Jones, Sammy Keith, Charles Lane, Randall Larson, Elizabeth MacRae, Scott Maiko, Albert and Ingrid Marhanka, Ronald and Deby Marhanka, Darren and Julie Marhanka, Joddie Marhanka, Kirstan Marhanka, Kaitlin Marhanka, Kerry Mcaleer (in Disney publicity), Larry McClain, Michael Miller, Shirley and Vic Mizzy, Ed Montagne, Ron Mueller, Jim Nabors, Leslie Nielsen, Tim Neely, Robert Pegg, Salvador Pequeño, Maggie Peterson, Jim Pierson, Bruce Plante, Joel Rasmussen, Barbara Rhoades, Dan Roebuck, Aaron Ruben, Gino Salomone, Bob Satterfield, Ray Savage (thanks for the incredible title!), Daniel Schweiger, Hal Smith, Joan Staley, Lin Steffanus, Fredrick Tucker, Allan Welch, Jeff Welch, Frank Welker, Taylor White, Dave Woodman, Francey Yarborough, and the Firefighters of the Riverview Fire Protection District in Missouri.

Special thanks to all the wonderful folks at Cumberland House Publishing, especially Ron Pitkin, Mary Sanford, Ed Curtis, Paul Mikos, and Paige Lakin.

Special thanks go to these generous organizations for research materials, photographs, images, and support: Walt Disney Productions, TV Land, Warner Brothers Studios, MCA/Universal, NBC-Universal, CBS Television, *TV Guide, Life* magazine, Hanna-Barbera Productions, Academy of Motion Pictures Arts & Sciences, Eddie Brandt's Saturday Matinee, United Artists, MGM Home Entertainment, Turner Classic Movies, Turner Home Entertainment, Percepto Records (percepto.com), 20th Century-Fox, New Line Cinema, Morgan Creek Productions, Filmation Associates, New World Pictures, and Columbia Records.

Introduction

I just knew that Don Knotts missed the movie role of a lifetime when the film *Mr. Magoo* was released in 1997. Someone—no one wants to admit who—cast comic actor Leslie Nielsen in the starring role of the myopic cartoon curmudgeon. While Nielsen can be hilarious in his own element and in the right vehicle, this was not it; the film fell flat faster than you could say "Road hog!"

As Don Knotts got older, his cartoonish face began to resemble old man Magoo with a bulbous nose, doughy cheeks, eyes that squinted a little (he actually did suffer from diminishing sight), and a balding head. You wanted to pet his head. He walked quietly like Magoo, with an overall cheerful glee like Magoo. If you ever caught him on a day without his toupee (he wasn't fooling anybody), when he was relaxed, you would know what I'm talking about. I know Don Knotts could have summoned a Jim Backus–like mumble for Magoo's vocals, and with the whole nervous-bundle bit, it would have been the ultimate cap on a beautiful movie career. Well, some things are better left to the imagination, I guess.

I must say, I had the good fortune of meeting this talented fellow, one of my TV idols, for the first time when he wasn't wearing the toupee or French cap. It was at a charity event in Santa Barbara, California, at which he took the stage with some of his *Steve Allen Show* contemporaries and performed for a sold-out theater. Don did his nervous weatherman routine, and it was as fresh and perfectly timed as the night he premiered it in the 50s on live television.

That night, when posing for a picture with the incredible Mr. Knotts after the show, I asked him politely if he would do a "scare take." He said, "Oh, sure," and instructed the photographer to click the shot "on three." He knew exactly what I wanted. I thought I'd join him in the moment and once I saw the Polaroid, I thought we looked like two deer caught in the headlights on a country road. Again, he knew how to time it just right to please a fan. That's the way he was with fans, always unassuming, quiet, and obliging. When he signed a photo from *The Ghost and Mr. Chicken* for me, I told him it was one of my favorites. I asked if he'd draw a little ghost next to his signature there . . . and he did it! He knew I was a fan.

I wish the timing of this book had been right and Don could have seen it come to fruition. I saw Don many times in the coming years and interviewed him with more than casual interest in his career. These films of his meant something to me; they threw me back to my

Don with coauthor Steve Cox.

childhood in the most pleasant of ways and they helped me learn about comedy technique. I enjoyed them all, no matter how many times I would see them. Ultimately, I'm not sure Don believed that a book about his film career would ever come to fruition. My coauthor and I had been working on this for many years, gathering interviews and photographic elements. We just never expected Don to leave us so suddenly.

The last time I saw Don was just a few months before he died of lung cancer in early 2006. It was the fall, right around Halloween, because I distinctly recall the pumpkins and spooky decorations in the Albertsons grocery store in Van Nuys that sunny afternoon. I went to get a flu shot at the temporary clinic they set up one afternoon at the grocery store—one I'd never been to before—and was shocked to see who was in front of me in line to get a shot. It was Don Knotts.

"Don . . . I heard you and Francey got married—congratulations!" I couldn't help but be surprised to see him and his young wife in line to get a flu shot at the grocery store, but I guess even TV idols want to ward away viruses. The setting was just a little odd, you know?

Although there were reports that he and his live-in girlfriend had married years prior, in reality, they only recently tied the knot. His wife, Francey, was taking good care of him here at the flu clinic line, even carrying a handy collapsible chair to be used in case the line was going to be long, and lovingly helping him off with his blue sweater when it was his turn. We talked for a few minutes while the process began, even through the shot, the bandage, and all. I think I was a nifty distraction for him because he didn't look at the needle even once. Don mentioned he'd recently recorded lines for an animated film called *Chicken Little* and he was enthused about that. We said our good-byes and I patted his hump. I couldn't wait to call my buddy Kevin Marhanka in St. Louis and tell him who I'd just run into. How bizarre it was. (I was imagining Don jumping out of his seat, screaming, bug-eyed, when the nurse hit him with that needle . . . now that would have been hilarious.) I was so distracted, I didn't notice the needle either. It was one of the more pleasant injections I've had to suffer in recent memory.

Just a few months later, Don Knotts was suddenly gone. He must have known he had lung cancer at the time, but only those very close to him were aware. I thought, *My God . . . I just saw him and he looked fine.* Nobody was more surprised than me when the news hit that he'd died in a hospital here in Southern California. That was a sad day.

* * *

There are many reasons to pay tribute to Don Knotts with a book like this. Quantity of films is not one of them. He made fewer than forty films in his career. Accolades never accumulated, as his films never earned the Academy's golden boy. As film successes go, his product never reaped riches like some of his comedy contemporaries'. But they were popular and successful, no question about that. If for nothing more than a career really well done, homage is due.

Don has said his favorites from his childhood were Laurel and Hardy and Abbott and Costello. Jack Benny was his idol, he admitted on more than one occasion. And yet, Knotts has been credited with performances on the level of silent comedy geniuses like Stan Laurel, Buster Keaton, and Harold Lloyd. His comedy is as memorable and brilliant from the silver screen as his predecessors' in film hilarity. No one has ever accused Don Knotts of stealing his style from anyone. He created his own characterizations. His characters have been rich and complex, winning him multiple Emmy Awards for bringing to life a man named Barney Fife. He made it all look so easy and by the time it was all said and done, he'd left us a career filled with some remarkably brilliant comedic moments, specifically in *The Ghost and Mr. Chicken* and *The Incredible Mr. Limpet.* Who hasn't laughed at his brief but hilarious turn in *It's a Mad, Mad, Mad, Mad World,* with Phil Silvers at his side? And although he established himself as a TV icon decades ago during *The Andy Griffith Show* years, his films have developed into cult outings, with millions of followers who can't get enough of the spastic star. Knotts was proud of the fact that his films were family attractions—a reason

" . . . one look at his beanpole-thin frame, his Silly Putty facial expressions, seemingly lifted from a Tex Avery cartoon, and, of course, those trademark ah-oooo-gah bug eyes makes you lose it. Even when Don Knotts doesn't mean to be funny, he just is. "

—Chris Nashawaty,
Entertainment Weekly,
October 1998

Disney Studios hired him time and again. About as naughty as he ever got was a few brief scenes in *The Love God?* that had him getting hilariously and endearingly seduced and sauced at the same time.

In Knotts's obituary in *Entertainment Weekly,* writer Ken Tucker put his unique brand into perspective this way: "So much of what we manage to keep contained inside ourselves—that roiling mess of nervousness, doubt, and barely controlled dread—Don Knotts had the courage and creativity to present as his *outer* self-image. Few comic actors have mined pent-up neurotic chaos as thoroughly as Knotts. . . ."

It's interesting to note that a succession of generations relate to Don Knotts for different reasons and varying characters. The older generation remembers him from his live, early days with Steve Allen on fuzzy black-and-white television screens. Some recall him as Barney Fife carrying the single bullet and also remember his movies from the 60s like *The Love God?* Perhaps a later generation identifies him explicitly as scarf-wearing Ralph Furley from TV's *Three's Company*; they can see him as none other than the nerdy landlord who hounded Jack Tripper and the girls for the rent money. His career is like one of Aunt Bee's homemade apple crumble pies: no matter how you divvy it up, there's something good in every slice. Barney Fife was just a mere blip in his career. A long and memorable blip, yes. But his movies deserve some recognition as more than cute family fare. Maybe his pinnacle in motion pictures, *The Ghost and Mr. Chicken* stands tall as a cult classic without peer. His film collaborations with Tim Conway mirror comedy gold in the tradition of Laurel and Hardy's silliness.

My friend and coauthor Kevin Marhanka decided one day—many years ago, I can't even recall exactly when—to combine our varying interests in Don Knotts and collaborate on a book about the man and his legacy of films. The project has melded quite well. We feel that we've created a nice tribute to Knotts here, and we hope you will enjoy it as much as we loved assembling it. We know we're not the only unabashed Don Knotts fans out there. There are legions.

A fresher crop of comedy giants have praised Knotts as a genius in his field. Appreciation for Knotts's style has only gained momentum. Unabashed fans of his work, including Jimmy Kimmel, Jim Carrey, Andy Dick, Conan O'Brien, and David Spade, have all been dubbed "disciples of Don," openly admitting they have been influenced by his work in television and film. John Ritter was a professed fan of the man who praised him in front of the press when Don Knotts received his star on the Hollywood Walk of Fame in January 2000.

Maybe this book will offer you a different perspective on the Don. The fact that he hated his middle name, Jesse, and that his friend Andy Griffith always called him Jess out of fun and affection provides a little insight into what good pals they really were, just like Andy Taylor and Barney Fife. Wouldn't we all be better off with a lifelong friend like that?

—Stephen Cox
Los Angeles, California

* * *

Nervous, scared, and shaking. Although these are great descriptions of Don Knotts in any of his films, it also describes me to a T as I was about to meet the man himself for the first time.

As a child growing up in the 1970s there never was a time that I thought I would get to meet my favorite comedian of all time, even though I dreamed of it. It was just something that seemed impossible. My earliest recollection of appreciating his style of comedy comes from the reruns of his hit shows, characters like Barney Fife and Ralph Furley. But then one day I had the chance to see a little film called *The Ghost and Mr. Chicken.* I loved it. To me, it was the epitome of his comic style, and it made me want to see more of this funny guy who got laughs for being nervous, scared, and shaking.

So meeting Don in April 1993, while living in Omaha, Nebraska, was something memorable for me. He was touring in the play *Last of the Red Hot Lovers* with another television icon, Barbara Eden, at the Orpheum Theater. I immediately decided to purchase tickets for my wife, Joddie, and me with hopes of maybe meeting him after the performance. The anticipation I had for the weeks prior was just pure joy, just knowing I was going to see Don perform live right in front of my eyes.

The show was funny, but as soon as it was over it was all about my personal quest to meet him. My wife knew how eager I was. We decided to wait around after the show and ended up just walking backstage at the theater. There was a group of about twenty-five people backstage waiting for a "meet and greet" opportunity with Don and his costar. (It's amazing what you can get away with if you act

Don with coauthor Kevin Marhanka.

like you belong somewhere.) My nerves were starting to get to me knowing Don was coming out of his dressing room shortly. Finally the moment arrived and everyone in the room clapped for the stars. There he was, a few feet away.

Don took a seat at a table and a line formed to say hello and talk with him. My turn arrived and all I could think about was . . . *Here is nervous Luther Heggs in front of me. What should I say?* I told Don how much I loved *The Ghost and Mr. Chicken* and he seemed to genuinely appreciate that. He was truly a nice person. I asked him to autograph a few things and he graciously took a picture with me. He thanked me again after I told him how much his career had meant to me. As I walked away all I could think of was that this surreal, incredible moment in my life would be cherished forever.

Well, this meeting prompted me to become a connoisseur and collector of Don Knotts's work. Granted, I'd always loved his films. Back in the '70s most people did not have VCRs to record their favorite programs. So what was a kid to do back then? The only thing I knew was to grab a tape recorder and record *audio* of a film or TV show. As a youngster, I would lie in bed at night just listening to the audiotape of *The Ghost and Mr. Chicken* and picturing the visuals in my mind. I'd hear all those funny lines in my sleep.

At some point I decided to start collecting Don Knotts memorabilia, especially things from his Universal films. I began with the movie posters, and it was a scavenger hunt. Those were the days before eBay. You actually had to attend collector shows or find little shops that sold those kinds of things, flea markets, nostalgia shows, etc. From then on I would discover things here and there, but not effortlessly; it wasn't until the mid- to late '90s that I discovered the Internet and eBay. This allowed the world of collecting, for me anyway, to fully bloom and provide access to all types of memorabilia. With the help of eBay I was able to locate the ultimate collector's piece, an actual 16mm Cinemascope film print of *The Ghost and Mr. Chicken.* It was like the holy grail of movies for me. Once I received it, I was going to actually see the movie in widescreen, the way it was meant to be viewed. It had never been aired on television in its original form, always chopped and edited. This really opened up the movie for me. There was so much more of the actual picture than people realized.

Years later, during vacations to Los Angeles, I had the opportunity to meet many people who worked with Don. It always seemed to center around my favorite film. I had the opportunity to meet character actor Charles Lane at his home (he played the attorney Mr. Whitlow in *Ghost*); I remember watching him chain-smoke and thinking how amazing that was considering he was in his nineties and hadn't quit yet. Another thrill was meeting writer Everett Greenbaum at his home, and asking him to yell out his famous line from the film: "Attaboy, Luther!" right into my video camera. He asked me, "Does that thing have sound?" Priceless.

I also visited Vic Mizzy, the musician who scored most of Don Knotts's Universal films, and begged him to play all the great music from *The Ghost and Mr. Chicken* on his Wurlitzer organ. That was a definite treat. (He obliged, too, because he appreciated those who recognized his music.) What great and unbelievable experiences I've been blessed with, and more than that, I have wanted to share this with other fans of Don Knotts for so long.

A few years later another opportunity came to see Don at a rare personal appearance at an autograph signing in Hollywood. The morning of the show Don was, I am sure, not prepared for what was going to hit him that day. Back in those days, celebrities charged about five dollars per autograph, and some would even sign your own things for free if you purchased a photo from them. Well, I must have had thirty or more items for Don to inscribe that day. It was a bargain. Don's line at this event never diminished; it was out the door all day long.

He looked quite tired as the afternoon approached. When I finally got up to him with all my things he was impressed with the collection of memorabilia I had for him to autograph: vintage movie posters, *TV Guide*s, rare photos, his comedy LP album from the '60s. These were just some of the interesting items. He would lift his glasses and examine the items closely and decide a good place for his signature. I especially remember him autographing my original *Reluctant Astronaut* poster. The image shows Don as an astronaut, floating nearly upside down in space. He signed it boldly right across his ass. His girlfriend, Francey, looked at it and laughed, saying, "Don . . . you have no shame." It was quite comical.

In 2000, I received a phone call from my friend (and co-author) Steve Cox, asking if I would like to come to Los Angeles for a Hollywood Star Ceremony. He'd been invited by TV Land, the sponsor of the event. Naturally I asked who it was for. He replied, "Don Knotts." I immediately told him my schedule was clear. "Just tell me when." *Nothing* was going to keep me away from that.

Steve and I decided to gear this trip around Don Knotts and related activities in order to assemble a book. We went to Uni-

versal Studios to go on the famous tour and see the original house used in *The Ghost and Mr. Chicken*. Sure enough, it was still there; it had changed quite a bit but was still somewhat recognizable. We decided to attempt to locate Joan Staley, who had costarred with Don in *Ghost*, and we were successful. She was a lovely woman (once a *Playboy* model) who adored Don and was gracious in sharing her memories of filming our favorite movie. We had lunch with her and joked about "having chicken noodle soup with Alma." (You gotta see the film.)

The Hollywood Chamber of Commerce and TV Land chose a beautiful sunny day in January 2000 to induct Don into the elite group of recipients of a star on the Hollywood Walk of Fame. Steve and I got there early and found a good spot to stand and take pictures. A small crowd had already formed in the area around the podium where Don would unveil his star. It wasn't long until some of Don's family and costars began to arrive. Then the moment arrived when both Don and Andy Griffith were escorted to the site inside an old police squad car, something right out of Mayberry. On hand for the ceremony were Don's *Three's Company* costars John Ritter and Jennilee Harrison. His *Andy Griffith Show* cohorts Howard Morris, Betty Lynn, producer Aaron Ruben, and Ronnie Schell were there, and, of course, Louis Nye from the *Steve Allen Show* days.

A ton of media were present, lined up in a barrage, waiting to cover the event. John Ritter and Andy Griffith both spoke about Don at the podium, and finally Don knelt down (with a little help) and unveiled the shiny star that bore his name. We cheered him on as did a nice crowd that had gathered to witness the honors.

We were invited to the private luncheon for Don hosted by TV Land. It was held at the posh Four Seasons Hotel, which was decorated inside like a country picnic, complete with checkered table cloths and fried chicken and the trimmings. Instead of being served, everyone passed around the plates of homemade food at the tables, just like an old-fashioned dinner setting. What a perfect theme. Luckily, Steve and I grabbed seats at a table that ended up being next to Don and Andy, and we got to see these two old friends enjoying their day together with their wives and friends. You could hear Andy making that familiar comment "Mmmm mmh! . . . Good food!" as he shoveled in the homemade mashed potatoes and gravy.

The real fun began when guest speakers took to the podium and began paying tribute to Don, sharing some great stories. John Ritter gave the best speech of all. It was heartfelt and warm, and you could tell how much he really appreciated Don and his comedic style. He said he learned so much from Don when working with him side by side on *Three's Company*. At one point, Don and Andy got up and performed a spontaneous duet together at the mike, which actually sounded pretty good. Then, Don spoke alone at the podium and sincerely thanked everyone for the day. At just the right moment, Steve yelled out, "Attaboy, Don!" and the audience laughed—even Andy chuckled.

Following a hearty dessert, there was some social time. Don was such a quiet and humble man who, you could see, was soaking in the attention that day. His two kids were there with him, and even his old army pal, Al Checco. There was a twinkle in his eye as he spoke with us and others around. I kept thinking, wow, what a special occasion this was for me to help celebrate his spectacular career.

Let's fast-forward to 2006. The news of the death of Jesse Donald Knotts really hit me. No one knew he was that ill, except his family. The news arrived and I suddenly felt emptiness. I was not sure what to feel at first. All of my memories began to flow through my mind; I felt the world had lost a true comedy genius. As I sat and reflected on this incredible loss I thought back on the time when I saw Don at what became his final appearance at a nostalgia show, signing autographs and greeting fans in 2005. I got to see and talk a little about his films and took a photo of him. As I got ready to take the picture of this comedy legend—just him sitting there—I asked if he would oblige and humor me with one last favor. I said, "Don, would you give me a scare take?" Without hesitation, he went right into that classic expression, reminding me of why I love this guy so much. This image irresistably became our back cover. What a great memory for me, my final time seeing him. His humorous facial expressions, comic timing, and wonderful comedic delivery were one of a kind. That's what I brought home . . . knowing Don as a kind, courteous man, great to all of his fans over the years. And just an overall nice guy.

Mainly known for his spectacular television career, his movie career has been sadly overlooked. Now is the time to change that and examine his incredible film career and pay proper respect to his work.

—KEVIN MARHANKA
ST. LOUIS, MISSOURI

"That's what I get for crash-landing into a civilization that worships Don Knotts. You don't? Well, you should. The man's a genius."

—ALF, FROM TV's *ALF,* 1986

The Incredible

MR. DON KNOTTS

> " His first name was Jesse. He never liked that name. He let me know it one time and I always called him Jess after that. "
>
> —ANDY GRIFFITH

Chock-Full o'Knotts

Maybe the greatest career challenge for Don Knotts came early in 1964, when he faced a serious crossroads. While his fame was skyrocketing, his shelves were filling up with awards, and his wallet was fat, he wasn't sure what to do next. Like a frazzled Barney Fife, he was all over the place, in the middle of the street with horns honking at him and cars whizzing by.

Knotts told veteran Hollywood columnist Hedda Hopper in January of that year that he had a "tough decision to make." Committed as a resident of Mayberry for one more year, Knotts wasn't sure where to turn after that. He was welcome to stay in town or head out on his own. It was his choice.

"I've had several offers to do my own show when I'm free, but I don't know where to jump. If I had a hit show the financial gain would be great; but there are many things to think about. I was on TV with Steve Allen four years, then this present series will make nine years straight on TV.

"My only Broadway experience was two years in *No Time for Sergeants,* and I'd like to do another play. Most of all I'd like to do an English comedy; I love their sense of humor. There's been some interest in that direction, but I haven't done anything about it as I'm committed to *Andy* for another year; I don't want to tie myself down so I won't be able to do feature pictures. Film offers don't always come in at the right time; you can't depend on the timing. They make such attractive offers for TV, but I think maybe if I took a year or two off to do some of these other things they wouldn't want me anymore."

During the hiatus before his final season, Don and his longtime pal—and boss—Andy Griffith took to the road and performed some routines together at Harrah's in Lake Tahoe. Promoters for the popular state fair circuit were slinging huge dollar signs their way to do a traveling Mayberry act on the road, but Knotts refused. The cast of *The Beverly Hillbillies* cashed in doing their arena show and so did cast members from *McHale's Navy,* as well as other popular TV performers. Admitting the money was fantastic and very hard to turn down, Knotts said at the time, "I grew to dislike state fairs some years ago when I was doing a radio show and they made me play them. I don't like working in an open arena with thousands in the audience. I enjoy getting applause if I do something good and move people, but it's different to get it because you're some freak from Hollywood the crowd is getting to look at."

Of course, as we know, Don took the route of feature films and bade farewell to Mayberry at the end of his phenomenal fifth season on the CBS sitcom. Everyone was sorry to see the pipsqueak bumbler make his exit. On the final day of filming, Don cleared out his dressing room, and with him he took the wooden sheriff's chair from the courthouse set and kept it as a memento. (He had it in his own personal home office until he died.) Everyone was sorry to see Don leave, especially his pal, "Ange."

Andy Griffith remembers that unpleasant period of time all too well, possibly because the show noticeably fizzled with the absence of Don's manic energy. "This may sound strange from a man to another man, but I loved Don, and when he left, I missed him very, very much, and I knew there'd be a hole in our show, but I knew there'd be a hole in my life, too. I missed him so dreadfully, I can't tell you. When Don left, the show lost its heart and soul."

Fans remember the change, too. The show turned to color, but the anguish on Andy Griffith's face showed shades of hazy gray. Most anyone who has followed *The Andy Griffith Show* will attest: the "color Andys," as some call them, are the most dreadful of the series' run. The star himself took on a meaner disposition and rarely smiled, rarely displayed the natural rural charm that was so welcome in American homes for years before. Andy Griffith's delivery turned predominantly disapproving in most episodes, an about-face from the encouraging, kind sheriff and father we'd grown accustomed to. The

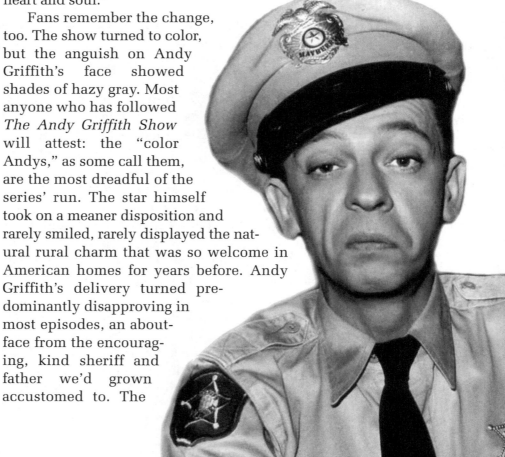

wind was knocked out of the show. "It stayed on for three more years," Griffith says, "and was in fact in first place for the whole last year that it was on, but it lost its heart when Don left."

For Knotts, his life's dream of becoming a bona fide movie star was about to blossom in full, glorious Technicolor form.

Knotts and Bolts

His given name was Jesse Donald Knotts, born on July 21, 1924, to William Jesse and Elsie Lusetta (née Moore) Knotts in Morgantown, West Virginia. Young Jesse preferred to be called Don, and early on this name stuck with at least his friends—family often used his given name.

Don's upbringing was anything but typical. He enjoyed the small-town existence that Morgantown gave him with school and friends, but his family life was anything but conventional. His father had suffered a severe nervous breakdown before Don was born, and the disability left him bedridden for much of the remainder of his life. During the depression, Don's mother supported the family, which included two older boys, Sid and William (nicknamed "Shadow"). One brother was ill with severe asthma and lung problems, while the other was an alcoholic. The family lived in a large, old house, and his mother rented rooms out to boarders and students from nearby West Virginia University. Don slept in the kitchen. He was, as the entire family was, always on the alert for renters who attempted to skip out before paying at the end of their stay.

Young Jesse Knotts, aspiring ventriloquist and actor.

He rarely looked back at his childhood years with any pride. "I felt like a loser," he told the *Los Angeles Times* in a 1976 interview. "I was unhappy, I think, most of the time. We were terribly poor and I hated my size."

When Don was in his early teens, he purchased a ten-cent gadget that was advertised to teach you to "Throw Your Voice!" with instructions on how to become a ventriloquist and thrill your friends and family. As a huge fan of ventriloquist and radio star Edgar Bergen and his dummy, Charlie McCarthy, it was a natural progression for this skinny small-town kid to take up performing. His mother helped pay for a wooden dummy from a department store, and Don honed his talents with his dummy, whom he named "Danny." Don performed at service club meetings and school gatherings, using his own material, he used to boast, and "some material stolen from Edgar Bergen." Even at that young age, Don knew he wanted to be an actor or performer of some kind. "I never thought about being anything else," he said. "My mother was a great movie fan and she used to take me with her a lot."

An average student, Don was slight in frame, small and wiry; some classmates called him "Spider." He attempted athletics but without much success. He played basketball, and he even tried boxing for one bout, but he knew it wasn't for him. "I was in the semi-finals of intramural wrestling in high school, and my opponent picked me up and mopped the mat with my face. My nose took a beating," he remembered. "When I walked in the house, my mother said, 'That's it. No more!'"

Don has credited his mother with being his greatest inspiration to follow his dream of making it big in show business. At seventeen, Don graduated from high school and left Morgantown to try his luck in New York with his ventriloquism act. He auditioned for the *Major Bowes Amateur Hour* on radio and the *Camel Caravan Radio Show,* but unfortunately he suffered rejection in both cases. Feeling like he failed miserably, he returned to Morgantown and enrolled in nearby West Virginia University as a speech major; his intention was to become a teacher and ultimately put his performing career on the back burner. Eventually, he was drafted into the army and sent to anti-aircraft school at Fort Bliss, Texas. Six months later, he reported to Fort Meade, Maryland, and auditioned for an army show, "Stars and Gripes," which was being created and cast.

Al Checco, a native of Pittsburgh, remembers meeting his old friend Don at the auditions for "Stars and Gripes," a new show written by Harold Rome. Both recruits had to audition for the famous Broadway impresario J. J. Shubert, who was also an officer in the military and in charge of assembling this show, which would travel the South Pacific and entertain the American troops.

"Being from Pittsburgh and Don was from Morgantown, well, in those days, you felt like you were neighbors," says Checco. "He and I got to talking and I happened to know the head of the drama school, Tippy Boyd, at West Virginia University where Don had gone to college. So we became friends very fast and both made the show." The entire "Stars and Gripes" company rehearsed for a few weeks and then shipped out to New Guinea at Milne Bay. "It was the rainy season, mud and slush and everything," recalls Checco. "After a week, our complexion was yellow from this Adaprine medication they gave us to ward off malaria.

"We did shows aboard ships and traveled around. We loved going on assignment to other places, especially for the navy, because they had better food like eggs, ice cream, stuff like that. Many shows we were bombed during performances because we were in the forward areas. Don and I both have more damned ribbons and gold stars because there for a while they'd bomb us every night and we'd have to stop the show."

Don relied on his skills as a ventriloquist to get hired on "Stars and Gripes," but, reveals Checco, he eventually grew to hate poor, wooden Danny. "He murdered his dummy. He threw it overboard. One day, we noticed that Danny was gone and Don just said, 'I don't know . . . we must have lost him.' Well, Don knew we couldn't just go out and buy a new one. The reason he got rid of him is because Don played a very clever stooge and he figured he'd be in a lot more sketches without the dummy. He did the Mister Frightened act even back then."

Checco remembers one special meeting during his years with the show. "Sometimes our paths would cross with the USO shows and we'd be a little bit farther behind the front lines and we could go and see a USO show. Jack Benny came to see our show; he saw Don and he fell in love with him. Don was a huge fan of Benny's too, and told him so." Little did Don dream that years down the line he would be guest-starring with Benny on one of his television specials.

Following his stint in the army, Don returned to Morgantown to complete his education. In his final year of college, he married fellow student Kay Metz. Don began postgraduate studies but eventually abandoned them. He and Kay borrowed a hundred bucks and headed to New York to try their luck in "the biz." It wasn't long after that that Don signed with a children's radio show called *Billy Benson and the B-Bar-B Riders,* in which he would perform as an old geezer named Windy Wales (who told tall tales). The radio show lasted five years, and during that time, Don needed to supplement his income so he auditioned again and landed jobs in television; he began playing characters on shows such as *Robert Montgomery Presents, Kraft Theatre,* and even a running role on the daytime soap opera *Search for Tomorrow* for one year. The next audition he went for would prove to change his life forever.

Don read for a role in an upcoming Broadway show called *No Time for Sergeants,* based on the best-selling novel by Mac Hyman. A young unknown named Andy Griffith was set to play the lead, Will Stockdale, a good-natured hick from the backwoods of Georgia who gets inducted and turns the army upside down. Don landed the dual role of an old preacher and an army officer who tests Stockdale for manual dexterity. The show opened in 1955 at the Alvin Theatre, and Don's role of the preacher opened the show and introduced the audience to Will Stockdale. The production was a hit, and eventually *No Time for Sergeants* was made into a feature film at Warner Brothers, in which both Andy Griffith and Don Knotts revived their characters for film audiences.

Remembers Griffith: "We became friends the second day of theater rehearsal for *No Time for Sergeants.* Don used to be in that radio

"Don Knotts is the most distinctive comic personality to emerge on the screen since Jerry Lewis. . . . *The Ghost and Mr. Chicken* proved to be enormously successful and achieved a level of rare Americana humor recalling the works of Leo McCarey, Frank Capra, and Preston Sturgess.**"**

—*VARIETY,* JANUARY 1967

show and I instantly recognized his voice. I knew that was him. I went up to Don and said, 'Ain't you Windy Wales?' And he was. And we became friends that day and that friendship lasted all these years."

During and after his run in *No Time for Sergeants*, Don was writing material and also performing on *The Garry Moore Show* during the day. It was on this show and eventually on *The Steve Allen Show* that he introduced his Nervous Man bit, a routine that would become a trademark for him. He based the character and physical delivery on an after-dinner speaker he once watched when he was young. Ten or fifteen years later, however, the Nervous Man would be one Don found hard to shed no matter how much he tried.

Life at home in 1962 with wife Kay, son Tommy, and daughter Karen.

Comedian Steve Allen hosted both *The Tonight Show* and a variety show of his own, with skits and sketches featuring a plethora of fantastic new talent: Louis Nye, Tom Poston, Bill Dana, Pat Harrington Jr., and, of course, Don Knotts. Eventually, Don moved to Los Angeles with Steve Allen's show in 1959. He and Kay had two children, a daughter, Karen, and a son, Thomas. The family lived primarily in the beautiful Glendale neighborhood in a home that was "perfect for children" he said. When the show left the air, he happened to have noticed Andy Griffith's pilot presentation, which was a segment airing on *The Danny Thomas Show* one evening.

"I saw Andy's pilot and I got the idea that maybe he should have a cowardly deputy," Knotts recalled. "So I called him and suggested the idea."

This was the birth of Barney Fife.

The Magic Bullet

At first, Don was signed for seventeen appearances on *The Andy Griffith Show,* which premiered in the fall of 1960. CBS's homespun situation comedy was set in the small town of Mayberry, North Carolina. Don was Deputy Barney Fife to Andy Griffith's Sheriff Andy Taylor. Since there was rarely any crime in Mayberry, the stories revolved mostly around the unique townsfolk and their relationships. The show became a runaway hit with audiences across America, and Mayberry was permanently and lovingly sewn into the nation's popular culture fabric.

Andy and Don developed a close working relationship over the

CLOCKWISE FROM TOP LEFT: Don and Frances Bavier holding their statues at the 1967 prime-time Emmy Awards. Don on Barney Fife: "He's childlike, is what he is. As a key, I think of a little boy, the way kids react so visibly. So I have Barney react visibly— but never with the cutes. I play him real."

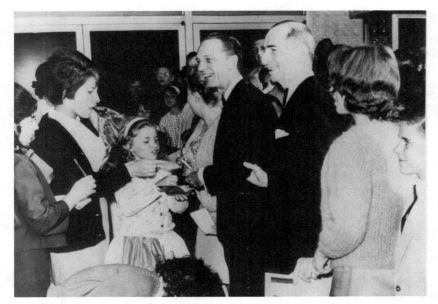

Don was never one to refuse a fan an autograph—especially kids.

years, working out their own routines and bits to complement each week's script. Andy Griffith has said that he would stand close to his costar, just inches away, and watch with amazement how Barney Fife would take life. "I could see it in his eyes, I could see Barney Fife come to life right in front of me," Griffith says. "Because Don was not like Barney at all. He was a different kind of guy, much more laid-back and calm."

Without a dash of doubt or jealousy, the show's star attributes the program's mass appeal to Barney Fife. "I think Don Knotts was the key to the success of the show," admits Andy Griffith today. "In the beginning, Don wasn't a part of the picture. I was supposed to be funny and tell little funny stories about the people in Mayberry. And when Don joined the show, by the second episode, I knew that Don should be funny and I should play straight for him. And that, I think, made the difference in the show. It gave us so much latitude. We could do all manner of stories that way."

Karen Knotts vividly recalls her father's dedication to the role and the series. On Sundays, the day Don set aside to learn his lines for the next week's episode, he would carefully mark his script and lock himself in his study to concentrate. Don was the type to act it out in privacy, yell his lines out loud as shrill as needed, pace, rant and rave, whatever the role required. The rule in the house was: No disturbing Dad.

"I used to sit outside the door and listen while he would take every line Barney had and practice it in probably, I would say, about thirty different ways," Karen recalls. "He tried different inflections, sometimes subtle changes. One word up with inflection, another word down inflected, until he found the way he wanted to read that line. Once he had it the way he wanted it, he would just repeat it over and over and over until it became locked in, and then he would put it together with the other lines. It was like a concert pianist learning a new piece. It was fantastic to hear how he would work so hard at that, and then of course when he got on the set, it was natural and real."

Academy Award–winning director Ron Howard, who grew up on the set of *The Andy Griffith Show* and learned his craft all the while, retains many vivid memories of his childhood spent on soundstages. "One of the vivid memories I have, one of the first images that come to mind is there on the set—Don creating one of the moments that he was going to play out on-screen—and Andy nearby with his head back just laughing," Howard recalls. "Don had a lot of admirers throughout his career and he earned every laugh, but I don't think there was a bigger fan than Andy. So many times I would see Andy with tears just streaming down his face laughing at something Don was creating, and the two of them were an amazing comedy team, and what they could generate was something historic."

During Don's five seasons on *The Andy Griffith Show* as the bullet-carrying deputy, he earned more than a handful of golden Emmy statues and endeared himself to millions of dedicated fans. Week after week he stole the show and became one of television's most popular personalities. "Around our fifth season, Andy said that he would not go beyond five seasons, so I started looking around for a job and landed a contract at Universal, a picture contract," said Knotts. "Then Andy turned around and decided to stay on the air. Earlier, I had asked Andy if we could team up for good, but he was too good an actor to want to do that. He shouldn't have and he didn't."

While Don's career was about to change, so was his married life. He and his wife Kay divorced in 1964. Without a mate, Don desperately sought stability in his life when both his hit show was gone and his marriage had crumbled. "Don was somewhat of a ladies' man," says his friend Al Checco. "He fancied himself something of a Frank Sinatra. The ladies loved him and he dated quite a bit, always had the ladies. They saw *something* in him."

Don did make a successful partner out of producer Ed Montagne, an Emmy Award–winning producer *(The Phil Silvers Show)* who was now making films at Universal. Montagne lured the comedian over to Universal to star in one feature film, and a subsequent feature-film contract would be contingent on the success of the initial release, *Running Scared.* In the initial production, retitled *The Ghost and Mr. Chicken,* Don would star as a jittery journalist bent on solving the mystery of a haunted house. The movie proved a huge hit at the box office and secured the comedian's next few years at the studio, not to mention a solid fan base with moviegoers. At Universal, he starred in a string of rather successful films—many were critically underrated at the time but have now achieved cult-classic status. On the heels of *Ghost,* Don starred in *The Reluctant Astronaut, The Shakiest Gun in the West, The Love God?,* and *How to Frame a Figg.*

Al Checco.

" He was Mr. Furley, Mr. Chicken and Mr. Limpet. But as Barney Fife, the shakiest gun in Mayberry, Don Knotts gave *The Andy Griffith Show*—and TV history—one of its most brilliant creations. "
—*TV GUIDE*, MARCH 2006

"Movies were something I never thought would happen to me," Knotts told *Entertainment Weekly* in 1998. "It's what I dreamed of as a kid. I'd have dreamed of a career in TV, but it wasn't around back then."

The Knotts vehicles were stacked with every great character actor in town (including several ex-Mayberry residents), excellent writing, and magical music created by Vic Mizzy. "Ed Montagne had used this little stock company of character actors in these films," explains Al Checco, who popped up in several Knotts films with his old army pal. "I never kissed his ass or asked him for work, because I was getting work, luckily. Much of our work together was coincidental, mainly because of Ed Montagne, who used to cast me in bit parts in Don's movies.

"I have a picture that Don signed to me years ago and he wrote: 'Long may our paths cross,'" says Checco. "What he meant by that is he was always surprised to see me in his movies, but it was all because of Ed Montagne. If Don recommended me for work, I wasn't aware of it. But then again, Don was a very compassionate guy. Years ago when I was in a show at the same time Don was in *No Time for Sergeants,* I lost my wife. She died at a very early age and we hadn't been married that long. It was tragic for me. Don was great, he practically saw me every night after the shows. I'd be crying in my booze and Don was there helping me through it, so concerned."

Nip It!

Karen Knotts described him as "an awesome father" who treated her more like a friend than a child. "He told me everything," she explained to Larry King on CNN in 2006. "Since a lot of my growing up he was single during the time, he talked to me about even his love life and everything that was going on. We were like buddies, like best friends.

"When my mother and he divorced, I went to live with him because she moved up to a ranch and I wasn't quite prepared for that. All through the '70s he was a single parent. He was quite the trendsetter during the '70s; he even had a man-purse and the whole thing. He was just a whimsical guy who had a lot of fun in his life."

In 1970, Don returned to television in a short-lived variety series, *The Don Knotts Show,* but it didn't work with audiences and the star was uncomfortable in that format. He continued to guest-star in other performers' shows *(Here's Lucy, The Captain and Tennille, The Muppet Show)* to earn a living and keep his exposure level up.

After a decade of doing the nervous routine on television and in films, the comedian was haunted by the little fellow with bugged eyeballs and pursed lips. Don sought to take his career and personal life in a different direction. He married Loralee Czuchna and remained quite content until their marriage ended nine years later. Careerwise, he took to the stage and toured in productions of Neil Simon's comedy *The Last of the Red Hot Lovers,* a snappy comedy called *The Mind with the Dirty Man,* and a production of *The Odd Couple* with Art Carney. Determined to adjust his public image and reinvent himself as an actor, Don told the press at the time: "The nervous little fellow who'd let big guys kick sand in his face is gone. I am branching out as a character comedian. I got the feeling of being boxed in, stuck with the same character, so I decided to do some theater because I could play parts there that I'd never be allowed to do on the tube."

When the Walt Disney Studios came calling for a TV special starring Mickey Mouse, Don was all ears. Eventually, he signed a contract with the studio to make a series of films; it was a welcomed departure that led to the inspired teaming of Knotts with fellow comedian Tim Conway in several films including *The Apple Dumpling Gang* and *The Apple Dumpling Gang Rides Again.* Don kept busy with more family-oriented feature films at Disney (*No Deposit, No Return* and *Herbie Goes to Monte Carlo*), as well as voice-over work and stage productions.

ABC Television approached Don in the summer of 1979 about joining the cast of the sexually revolutionized hit show *Three's Company;* Knotts leaped at the opportunity to return to prime time. He would be the landlord, replacing Norman Fell and Audra Lindley as the Ropers. As the ascot-wearing pseudo-swinger Ralph Furley, Don slipped into his toupee phase and played the goofy landlord to the hilt. Secretly nervous about performing in front of a live audience for the weekly tapings, Don soon shook his fears and blended well with costars John Ritter, Suzanne Somers, and Joyce DeWitt. Don stayed with the show until it went off the air in 1984 after eight seasons.

"When Don agreed to come on the show, we were absolutely astounded," says Joyce DeWitt, who played peppy Janet on the series. "That this amazing, creative, extraordinary talent would agree to join our cast.

"The first day he came to the set, we were dumbfounded," she remembers. "We could hardly speak because Don was working with us. He came in and thanked us for inviting him and asked for absolutely nothing. He was the kind of person you wanted to make sure was taken care of because Don would never ask for himself. He was such a gift to the show, making a seamless transition from the Ropers leaving and Mr. Furley coming in.

"One of the great joys for me about *Three's Company* that lives in

my heart always," DeWitt adds, "is that they gave Janet the job of dealing with Mr. Furley for the trio and quite often my scenes would be just Don and me together. That was a great gift that they gave me. I had no idea of the joy that being a straight man could be until I worked with Don. . . . You could just lay it out there and get out of the way. There were many nights that we had to stop camera and start over because he was so good and so funny. The freshness that he could do it each time was so disarming."

Mixed Knotts

As a self-described hypochondriac, Don complained of a host of ailments and neuroses over the years. And as it happened, he did suffer numerous health reversals in his later years. He was treated for macular degeneration, a condition that caused great loss in his vision and terribly limited his activities. Driving was out, and his ability to read scripts was hindered. He suffered with depression after his second marriage ended, and his health began to deteriorate—so much so that one tabloid reported he'd attempted suicide with an overdose of prescription medication. In an effort to cheer up his old pal, Andy Griffith hired him to make a few guest appearances on his popular TV show *Matlock* on NBC.

In the '90s Don met actress Francey Yarborough, thirty-plus years his junior, and the couple began dating and eventually living together and working side by side in stage productions. Never one to disappoint the fans, he made sure to include the "Barney Fife sniff" in each of his stage performances— something audiences loved. He knew that something as simple as a quick cocky remark followed by a sniff could bring down the house. Don once again enjoyed the applause of a theater audience when he toured in productions of *Last of the Red Hot Lovers* (with Barbara Eden), *Harvey,* and *On Golden Pond.* In his final run of *On Golden Pond,* he tore his Achilles tendon and had to wear a brace onstage. Even that injury failed to stop him from meeting his fans.

He began making personal appearances in the Midwest at nostal-

The cast of *Three's Company* celebrates the taping of its 150th episode on the Regal Beagle set (February 1983).

gia shows and *Andy Griffith Show* festivals and tributes. Fans greeted him in droves. In some venues, he performed a popular one-man show in which he reminisced about his entire career, introduced clips from his films and TV shows, and, of course, sent the audience into hysterics with the Nervous Man routine once again. He'd come full circle, and he was finally enjoying it.

Ron Howard recalls an experience on the set of the film *How the Grinch Stole Christmas!* in which his old costar received some fitting adulation. "It turns out that Jim Carrey is a huge Don Knotts fan and had imitated him in his act at one time and had even done him on an *In Living Color* sketch, and he could do a great Don Knotts," says Howard.

Andy and Don reunite on TV's *Matlock.*

"We were doing the Grinch and Jim had to wear this really oppressive makeup. It was really getting him down," he remembers. "He had to wear the green heavy Grinch costume and the prosthetic makeup and contact lenses. And the shooting went on and you could just see his energy was draining. One day, I surprised him by getting Don to come to the set. So Don showed up and it was a complete surprise to Jim Carrey. Jim was in his full Grinch costume standing up at the mouth of the Grinch's cave, which was this tall set at the top of a soundstage. He looked down and he squinted and he could see that it was Don and he went into a really brilliant Don Knotts imitation, and I only wish the cameras were rolling. Here he was in the Grinch costume doing Barney Fife. It was hilarious; and that day, Jim's spirits were really up because he got to go down and visit with one of his idols, and Don graciously spent an entire afternoon hanging around with Jim Carrey. That's the kind of guy Don was, very unassuming and very gracious."

As Don was nearing his eighties, fans were beginning to lay great praise on the comedian once again. A full-scale cultural renaissance of sorts was taking place . . . and he knew it. His well-received appearance in the 1998 film *Pleasantville,* starring Tobey Maguire, launched more work and exposure for the legendary performer. One magazine dubbed it "Knottsapalooza." In 2000, Don penned his autobiography, *Barney Fife and Other Characters I Have Known,* and received a star on the famous Hollywood Walk of Fame.

Don continued to do voice-over work for television and films

BUILD AND REPAIR WITH CONCRETE

THE COMPLETE DO-IT-YOURSELF MANUAL

SECOND EDITION
EXPANDED & UPDATED
NEW PROJECTS & PRODUCTS!

DON KNOTTS SAYS:
"If I can do it, YOU can do it!"

Never one to turn down work, Don lent his image to be used on the cover of a how-to book about working with concrete.

(*Cats Don't Dance, Chicken Little, Air Buddies*); it was a job he relished since he didn't have to memorize lines and could take his time in the studio with little pressure. He kept busy, but in late 2005 his health took a turn for the worse and he was diagnosed with lung cancer; he kept the grave news from even his closest friends. Sadly, he was forced to cancel a trip to his hometown of Morgantown for a tribute festival as he started chemotherapy and his energy was zapped. His third wife, Francey, whom he'd married just months before the diagnosis, took loving care of the actor in his decline. On February 24, 2006, while at home in his West Los Angeles condominium, Don's oxygen levels began to become erratic and he was rushed to UCLA Medical Center.

"He died about eleven o'clock that night at UCLA," revealed Andy Griffith to host Larry King on CNN. His old friend was one of the last to see him. "I was with him until six or six-thirty, I guess. He couldn't respond. I was able to tell him I loved him. I asked him to breathe . . . keep breathing, Jess. We were down in the emergency room and we were near enough we heard the doctor tell Francey, Don's wife, that his heart had stopped in the ambulance and they had brought him back."

Andy and Don's family had known the end was near. Don Knotts died of pneumonia, a result of the end stage of lung cancer. He was eighty-one years old.

The news of Don Knotts's death shocked a nation of admirers. An old classic had made his exit from the stage—this time for good. It was a sad day for millions of Mayberry fans and for comedy fans alike. Across the country, newspaper and magazine editorial cartoonists couldn't help but pay fitting tribute in the most comical of ways. Many of the editorial cartoons similarly featured Barney Fife at the pearly gates with Saint Peter asking him to surrender his bul-

SARAH? GET ME AUNT BEE. TELL HER BARNEY'S HERE FOR DINNER

let. One artist drew a dignified sketch of Barney Fife, in uniform, clutching his police hat in his hands. The inscription simply read: Officer Down.

Respect for the Don

- A Veteran of World War II, Jesse Donald Knotts was awarded the Victory Medal, Philippine Liberation Medal, Asiatic-Pacific Campaign Medal (with four bronze service stars), Army Good Conduct Medal, Marksman Badge (with Carbine Bar), and an Honorable Service Lapel pin.

- Don Knotts won an astounding five Emmy Awards from the Academy of Television Arts & Sciences for his performances on *The Andy Griffith Show*. All Emmy Awards were for "Outstanding Performance by an Actor in a Supporting Role in a Comedy." Knotts won in 1961, 1962, and 1963 as a series regular. In 1966, he won for his single performance as a guest star in the episode "The Return of Barney Fife." The next year, he again won for his guest-starring turn in the episode "Barney Comes to Mayberry."

- Former West Virginia Governor John D. Rockefeller honored Don in 1982 with a large certificate naming him a "Distinguished West Virginian."

- In 1994 former Monongalia County Sheriff Joseph C. Bartolo (Morgantown, West Virginia) appointed Don "Honorary Deputy Sheriff of Monongalia County."

- In January 2000, Don Knotts was awarded a star on the famous Hollywood Walk of Fame located at 7083 Hollywood Boulevard. This honor was for his contributions in the field of television. The cable network TV Land sponsored the nomination and subsequent installation of the actual star.

- On January 4, 2000, the A&E network premiered their *Biography* documentary about the comedian titled "Don Knotts: Nervous Laughter," narrated by Peter Graves.

Don received multiple Emmy Awards for his performance as Barney Fife.

- The University of Kansas (Lawrence, Kansas) Theatre Department established the New Theatre Guild Don Knotts Scholarship, which is awarded "to a full-time undergraduate and graduate student in good standing."

- The TV Land Awards honored Don in 2003 as winner in the category of "Favorite Second Banana." In 2004, Don and the rest of the surviving main cast of *The Andy Griffith Show* were honored with the "Legend Award" from TV Land.

- Morgantown, West Virginia, helped Don celebrate his eightieth birthday in 2004. His

Miss Florida (Flora Jo Chandonnet) and Chief Billy Osceola (a Seminole Indian chief) present an honorary citizenship award to Don in Florida at the Weeki Wachee Springs premiere of *Limpet*.

hometown gave him a parade and honored him with the Don Knotts Film Festival the next summer. The naming of Don Knotts Boulevard in Morgantown was officiated with a ceremony. In 2007, following Don's death, the town established West Virginia's Walk of Fame, in front of the Metropolitan Theater on High Street (where he performed as a high school student), and his was the first star implanted in the walk.

" I've made about thirty movies and my favorite is **The Ghost and Mr. Chicken,** which was the first feature I did on my own after I left *The Andy Griffith Show,* and I had a lot of control over the writing and everything. And then another picture I liked was the one that Tim Conway and I got together on later at Disney, **The Apple Dumpling Gang.** And the other picture I'm proud of is **The Incredible Mr. Limpet.** "

—DON KNOTTS, ON HIS TOP THREE FAVORITES

The Movies

NO TIME FOR SERGEANTS

Released: 1958
Produced by: Mervyn LeRoy, Alex Segal
Written by: Mac Hyman (novel), Ira Levin (play and film), John Lee Mahin (film)
Directed by: Mervyn LeRoy
Running Time: 111 minutes
Warner Bros.

Cast

Andy Griffith (Pvt. Will Stockdale), Myron McCormick (Sgt. Orville C. King), Nick Adams (Pvt. Benjamin B. Whitledge), Murray Hamilton (Irving S. Blanchard), Howard Smith (Maj. Gen. Eugene Bush), Will Hutchins (Lt. George Bridges), Sydney Smith (Maj. Gen. Vernon Pollard), James Millhollin (Psychiatrist Maj. Royal B. Demming), Don Knotts (Cpl. John C. Brown/Manual Dexterity), Jean Willes (WAF Captain), Bartlett Robinson (Captain), Henry McCann (Lt. Cover), Dub Taylor (McKinney), William Fawcett (Pa Stockdale), Raymond Bailey (Base Colonel), Thomas Browne Henry (Senator), Jack Mower (Sheriff), Robert Sherman (Lt. James Miller), Malcolm Atterbury (Bus Driver), Benny Baker (Capt. Jim Able), Bill Baldwin (Announcer-Loudspeaker Voice), Dan Barton (Tiger), John Bradford (Radio Sergeant), Wade Cagle, John Caler, Robert Hover, David Carlisle, Sammy Jackson, Rad Fulton, James Westmoreland (Inductees), Robert Christopher (Reporter), Donald R. Clark (Guitar-Playing Inductee), John Close (Sentry), Francis De Sales (Sgt. TC Payne), Jamie Farr (Lt. Gardella), Paul Hahn (Corporal Attendant),

Peggy Hallack (Rosabelle McKinney), Clark Howat (Lieutenant), Robert F. Hoy, Fred Stromsoe, Ernie Taylor (Tough Guys), Jack Mann (Psychiatrist Corporal), Tom McKee (Charles—Aide), George N. Neise (Barker—Gen. Bush Aide), Mary Scott (Cigarette Girl), Robert Sherwood (Second Lieutenant), Bob Shield (Radio Announcer), Verne Smith (Announcer), Bob Stratton (Lt. Kendall), John Truax (Driver), Sailor Vincent (Fighter in Bar), Dick Wessel (Drunk Infantryman), Albert "Ace" Williams, Fred Coby (Sentrys)

Synopsis

A draft board agent swoops down on a small backwoods farm in Georgia and claims a naive hillbilly farm boy, Will Stockdale, for military service. Over his father's protest, Will confesses that he'd like to become a soldier and make something of himself. Also joining the inductees is nebbish Ben Whitledge, a wiry, high-strung kid with horn-rimmed glasses who wants to be an infantryman more than anything. Ben and Will become friends and help each other get through the arduous task of induction tests, questionnaires, and even barracks' brawls.

Sergeant King, who wants nothing more out of the air force than peace and quiet, realizes he must make sure Stockdale passes the tests—even if it means cheating. One of the examiners at the induction center, a tall, neurotic psychiatrist, tries to prove that good-natured Will is suffering from a series of neuroses, including a suppressed interest in the opposite sex.

Will Stockdale surprises everyone and rises to new heights as the efficient latrine duty officer. From gunnery school, Will and Ben are assigned to a bomber piloted by officers who were the lowest in their class. During a routine test mission, a tail section of the plane explodes and Will and Ben leap out and parachute to safety. It is assumed that the soldiers have been "lost" during the mission, so they are given honors posthumously at the base.

However, when Will and Ben make their presence known during the ceremonies, they are surprised when they have trouble convincing the brass they are actually who they say they are. In order to avoid great embarrassment, the general makes some hasty concessions in order to smooth over the mistake and keep Will and Ben content. The country bumpkin has outwitted everyone—from the latrine all the way up to the big brass.

Sidelights

- Look for character actors Raymond Bailey (Mr. Drysdale on TV's *The Beverly Hillbillies*) without his toupee and a young Jamie Farr (Klinger on TV's *M*A*S*H*) without a dress.
- *No Time for Sergeants* was adapted into a live "teleplay" on the program *The U.S. Steel Hour,* which aired on March 15, 1955, and was nominated for an Emmy Award. Later, in 1964, it inspired a sitcom on ABC-TV starring Sammy Jackson, but it lasted less than half a season. (Jackson appeared in the film version as an inductee.)
- In the Broadway stage version, Don Knotts played two roles: a preacher and Corporal Brown/Manual Dexterity.
- The almost painfully thin Don Knotts plays his role in this film as beautifully exasperated, chirpy, with an ultra-high-pitched tone that surpasses falsetto.
- Veteran character James Millhollin, who portrayed the confused psychiatrist, first won over audiences in this funny role in the original Broadway run and was asked to re-create the role for the film. Millhollin later worked with Don Knotts playing the hen-pecked banker in *The Ghost and Mr. Chicken* and also playing a dour funeral director in *How to Frame a Figg.*

Behind the Scenes

In October 1955 Andy Griffith faced audiences for the first time on Broadway in the comedy play *No Time for Sergeants,* at the Alvin Theatre. The six-footer with a smooth southern drawl had audiences roaring from the moment the first curtain came up. Young Don Knotts was in the production as well, along with up-and-coming actors Roddy McDowall and Van Williams.

Andy Griffith and Nick Adams star in *No Time for Sergeants* in 1958.

The production played several hundred performances and became a huge hit on Broadway.

Adapted from the best-selling novel by Mac Hyman, *Sergeants* is the hilarious tale of a backwoods farm boy who is drafted and, through sheer coincidence and innocence, outwits superiors and races his way to the top. The play propelled Andy Samuel Griffith to stardom, and he was offered the same role in the motion picture directed by Mervyn LeRoy. Andy Griffith, Myron McCormick, James Millhollin, and Knotts were the only

In his first film role, Don Knotts (Corporal Brown) tests Andy Griffith (Will Stockdale) for manual dexterity.

actors drafted from their Broadway roles and ordered to report to duty on the Warner Brothers soundstages for the film version. The film, which was an amalgam of material from the book and hit Broadway play, was a smash hit for Warner Brothers, with some critics praising it as better than both the book and the play.

Reviews

Hollywood Reporter: "Andy Griffith makes Will, the knuckle-domed hero, one of the most charming boneheads in military history."

Variety: "Griffith's experience with the base psychiatrist, admirably portrayed by James Millhollin, is one of the highlights of the picture. . . . Good performances in tone with the farcical quality of the picture are given by Murray Hamilton, Howard Smith, Will Hutchins, Sydney Smith, Don Knotts, and Bartlett Robinson as assorted enlisted men and officers."

WAKE ME WHEN IT'S OVER

Released: 1960
Produced by: Mervyn LeRoy
Written by: Richard L. Breen, Howard Singer
Directed by: Mervyn LeRoy
Running Time: 126 minutes
Warner Bros.

Cast

Ernie Kovacs (Capt. Charlie Stark), Dick Shawn (Gus Brubaker), Margo Moore (Lt. Nora McKay), Jack Warden (Doc Dave Farrington), Nobu McCarthy (Ume), Don Knotts (Sgt. Warren), Robert Strauss (Sam Weiscoff), Noreen Nash (Marge), Parley Bear (Col. Hollingsworth), Robert Emhardt (Joab Martinson), Marvin Kaplan (Hap Cosgrove), Tommy Nishimura (Pvt. Jim Hanigawa), Raymond Bailey (Gen. Weigang), Robert Burton (Col. Dowling), Frank Behrens (Maj. Bigelow), Linda Wong (Kaiko), Caroline Richter (Mrs. Hollingsworth), Robert Peoples (Connorton), Richard Tyler (Lt. William Pincus), David Bedell (Capt. Arthur Finch), Paul Comi (Lt. Bressler), Ashley Cowan (Greiner), Owen Cunnigham (Col. Geoffery Schmitt), Ralph Dumke (Sen. Gillespie), Tommy Farrell (Smitty), Bess Flowers (Hotel Extra), Alex Gerry (Lawyer Arnold), Ron Hargrave (Hawaiian Singer), Thomas Browne Henry (Investigating General), Jay Jostyn (Col. Mulhern), Mike Mahoney (Naval Commander), Gregg Martell (Navy Chief), Eugene McCarthy (Corp. Mike), Rollin Moriyama (Tanaka), Byron Morrow (Maj. Horace Tillman), Jimmy Murphy (Reagan), Scott Peters (Hagejos), Michael Quinn (Capt. John Guevara), Vin Scully (CBS Broadcaster), Larry Thor (TV Broadcaster), Carleton Young (Radar Instructor)

Synopsis

Gus Brubaker, a laid-back World War II air force veteran, has been rerecruited due to a mistaken identify and finds himself shipped off to a remote Pacific Island. At the tiny radio outpost on the island called Shima, he learns that the commanding officer is his old commander from the Eighth Air Force, Capt. Charles Stark, a screwball with little regard for military discipline.

While attempting to correct his mistaken rerecruitment, Brubaker learns that his transfer and discharge application is hopeless. In order to pass the time and earn some cash, Brubaker concocts a scheme to build a resort hotel on the island featuring the native girls and natural hot springs as an added attraction. The rest of the GIs on the island are all equal members of the new business venture, which becomes a huge success.

When word gets out to the states about the resort, an inspector general's team—along with a senator—is immediately dispatched to the island to conduct a full investigation. Brubaker is the subject of a court-martial and must defend himself. Stark, who has been transferred off the island, returns to testify for his old pal. The chaotic court session and deliberation finally find Brubaker innocent; a mistrial has been declared on the grounds that the wrong man had been tried.

Sidelights

- Filming was completed on March 17, 1960. The screenplay was developed from a novel by Howard Singer.
- The Los Angeles premiere was held at the Pantages Theatre on April 8, 1960.
- This is Don Knotts's second military comedy on film. Critic James Powers felt Knotts's performance was "another standout," and that he made his "few individual scenes hilarious."
- A convoluted military comedy filled with unconventional officers, this comedy has been compared to *Operation Petticoat* and *Mister Roberts.* For the most part, Don Knotts's role gets lost in the crowd.
- Look out for the voice of Ernie the Keebler Elf: actor Parley Baer (as Colonel Hollingsworth). Baer, a prolific radio, film, and television actor, also portrayed Mayor Stoner on *The Andy Griffith Show.*
- The main title song is performed by Andy Williams.

Reviews

The Hollywood Reporter:
"[Richard] Breen's screenplay spends too long getting into the story. The introductory passage isn't really necessary and it doesn't have any particular comic value of its own. The film gets going with real pace once it is

past this road block and [Mervyn] LeRoy lets loose some wacky subsidiary characters, Kovacs, Jack Warden, Robert Strauss, Marvin Kaplan, Tommy Nishimura, among others. Then it achieves, and mostly maintains a more than satisfactory farce tempo."

Variety: "The fascination of Richard Breen's screenplay lies in the writer's ability to resolve real absurdities into absurd realities without defeating either the humor or the drama of the story. On top of that, he has come through with dialog that is sharp and funny."

THE LAST TIME I SAW ARCHIE

Released: 1961
Produced by: Jack Webb
Written by: William Bowers
Directed by: Jack Webb
Running Time: 98 minutes
United Artists

Cast

Robert Mitchum (Archie Hall), Jack Webb (William "Bill" Bowers), Martha Hyer (Peggy Kramer), France Nuyen (Cindy Hamilton), Louis Nye (Pvt. Sam Beacham), Joe Flynn (Pvt. Russell Drexler), Del Moore (Pvt. Frank Ostrow), Jimmie Lydon (Pvt. Billy Simpson), Richard Arlen (Col. Edwin Martin), Don Knotts (Capt. Harry Little), Robert Strauss (Msgt. Stanley Erlenheim), Harvey Lembeck (Duty Sgt. Malcolm Greenbriar), Claudia Barrett (Lola), Theona Bryant (Daphne), Elaine Devry (Carole), Marilyn Burtis (Patsy Ruth), Howard McNear (Gen. Williams), Eugene McCarthy (Bartender), James Mitchum (Corporal), John Nolan (Lt. Oglemeyer), Nancy Kulp (Miss Willoughby), Don Drysdale (Soldier in E-Club), Bill Kilmer (Soldier), George Barrows (Soldier in Jeep), Dick Cathcart (Soldier), Robert Clarke (Officer), Martin Dean (Second Lieutenant), Phil Gordon (Soldier), Sam Harris (Restaurant Patron), Reed Howes (Bus Passenger), Donald Kerr (Street Car Conductor), Alan Reynolds (Major), Bill Idelson, Lillian Powell, Art Balinger, Robert Osborne (uncredited role; Army Air Force Pilot)

Synopsis

Nearing the end of World War II, a number of overage and overweight civilian pilots are drafted into the army air force to ferry aircraft and transport supplies. With the arrival of combat pilots rotated from the war zones, the older soldiers find themselves with little to do. Conniving Pvt. Archie Hall makes the best of his downtime by convincing noncoms and others on the base that he is a general and on a mission. Along with his partner in crime, Pvt. Bill Bower, the two begin spending most of their time off base at parties and pubs. They become well acquainted with a couple of ladies, Cindy and Peggy. Cindy is a Japanese-American who is eventually suspected by Hall and Bower as possibly being a spy for the enemy because she constantly gives them money. Unknown to them is that in reality she is a spy for the United States trying to unravel a spy ring. Archie eventually turns the tables and ends up receiving a medal out of the whole ordeal. After getting their discharge both Hall and Bower go to Hollywood and land jobs at a movie studio. After a while Bower becomes a successful screenwriter pounding the keys in a cubicle working on films, while goldbrick Archie wrangles his way into becoming head of the studio.

Sidelights

- Filming was completed on January 6, 1961.
- This film was fledgling director Jack Webb's most expensive production to date. The film cost nearly $2 million to produce; it was also his biggest flop, grossing just above half of its production cost.
- This is Don Knotts's third military comedy. His stints in the service fail to improve or expand as his role in this film is minuscule. In this film, he is a nervous (of course) commanding officer, Corporal Little of the 165th Squadron, U.S. Army Air Corps. He prefers to be known as "Ol' Iron Pants," but no one takes him seriously.
- Look for small roles from ballplayers Bill Kilmer of the San Francisco 49ers and Don Drysdale of the Los Angeles Dodgers. James Mitchum, the eldest son of star Robert Mitchum, has a small role in the film.
- Robert Osborne—author, film critic, and host on Turner Classic Movies—has a rare on-camera role as a feisty pilot. For some reason, Osborne goes uncredited in the film; and to this day, he does not make reference to the film on his own résumé.
- Watch for Eddie Quillan as the bellboy. Quillan hailed from the mid-1920s film era, including Mack Sennett comedies. He would play a bit part in several Don Knotts films including *The Ghost and Mr. Chicken, The Shakiest Gun in the West,* and *How to Frame a Figg.* Writers Greenbaum and Fritzell would also use him in their Andy Griffith film *Angel in My Pocket.* Coincidentally, his last film appearance would be an episode of *Matlock* titled "The Author" in 1987.
- Look for Mayberry's Howard McNear (Floyd the Barber) in a bit role.
- This film bombed at the box office. One critic from the *Hollywood Citizen News*

THE INCREDIBLE MR. DON KNOTTS

blamed Jack Webb: "Perhaps if Jack Webb had stuck to his directorial chores and left his 'buddy' role to someone else, things might have possibly turned out a little better."

Reviews

Hollywood Citizen News: "Theatergoers who might have expected an army comedy similar in slapstick theme to the excellent British releases of the same nature are in for a big disappointment. . . . It all seems rather an absurd waste of time and talent and an unhappy venture for all concerned."

Los Angeles Times: "The most irritating fact is that it could have been a really hilarious picture, but every time the action shows promise of better things to come, it bogs down in the same old static situations and these receive no help from William Brower's script or Jack Webb's direction."

Veterans of *The Steve Allen Show,* Don Knotts and Louis Nye appeared together in *The Last Time I Saw Archie.*

Captain Little (Don Knotts) introduces himself as "Ol' Iron Pants" to the squad.

IT'S A MAD, MAD, MAD, MAD WORLD

Released: 1963
Produced and Directed by: Stanley Kramer
Written by: William Rose and Tania Rose
Running Time: 192 minutes
United Artists

Cast

Spencer Tracy (Capt. C. G. Culpepper), Milton Berle (J. Russell Finch), Sid Caesar (Melville Crump, DDS), Buddy Hackett (Benjy Benjamin), Ethel Merman (Mrs. Marcus), Mickey Rooney (Ding "Dingy" Bell), Dick Shawn (Sylvester Marcus), Phil Silvers (Otto Meyer), Terry-Thomas (Lt. Col. J. Algernon Hawthorne), Jonathan Winters (Lennie Pike), Edie Adams (Monica Crump), Dorothy Provine (Emeline Marcus-Finch), Eddie "Rochester" Anderson (Cabdriver), Jim Backus (Tyler Fitzgerald), Ben Blue (Biplane Pilot), Joe E. Brown (Union Official), Alan Carney (Police Sergeant), Chick Chandler (Detective), Barrie Chase (Sylvester's Girlfriend), Lloyd Corrigan (Mayor), William Demarest (Chief Aloysius), Andy Devine (Sheriff), Selma Diamond (Ginger Culpepper Voice), Peter Falk (Cabdriver), Norman Fell (Detective), Paul Ford (Col. Wilberforce), Stan Freberg (Deputy Sheriff), Louise Glenn (Billie Sue Culpepper Voice), Leo Gorcey (Cabdriver), Sterling Holloway (Fire Chief), Edward Everett Horton (Mr. Dinckler), Marvin Kaplan (Irwin), Buster Keaton (Jimmy the Crook), Don Knotts (Nervous Motorist), Charles Lane (Airport Manager), Mike

Mazurki (Miner), Charles McGraw (Lt. Matthews), Cliff Norton (Reporter), Zasu Pitts (Gertie the Switchboard Operator), Carl Reiner (Tower Controller), Madlyn Rhue (Secretary Schwartz), Roy Roberts (Policeman at Garage), Arnold Stang (Ray), Nick Stewart (Truck Driver), The Three Stooges: Moe Howard, Larry Fine, and Curly-Joe DeRita (Firemen), Sammee Tong (Chinese Laundryman), Jesse White (Radio Tower Operator), Jimmy Durante (Smiler Grogan), Jack Benny (Man in Car in Desert), Paul Birch (Policeman), John Clarke (Helicopter Pilot), Stanley Clements (Detective), Howard Da Silva (Airport Officer/Patrolman), Roy Engel (Patrolman), James Flavin (Patrolman), Nicholas Georgiade (Detective), Stacy Harris (Police Radio Voice), Don C. Harvey (Policeman in Heli-

Driving madly in his 1956 Ford Fairlane Sunliner, Don Knotts takes abrupt orders from stranger Phil Silvers.

copter), Allen Jenkins (Police Officer), Robert Karnes (Police Officer Simmy), Tom Kennedy (Traffic Cop), Harry Lauter (Police Dispatcher), Ben Lessy (George the "Steward"), Bobo Lewis (Pilot's Wife), Jerry Lewis (Man in Car Who Runs over Hat), Bob Mazurki (Eddie the "Miner's Son"), Barbara Pepper, Charles Sherlock, Eddie Smith, Doodles Weaver, Minta Durfee, Lennie Weinrib (Additional Radio Voices)

Synopsis

A wacky group of road travelers rush to aid a dying con man whose car has jettisoned off the side of a mountain highway. They all witness the man's death, and his final words to the motorists are clues on how to locate a treasure of $350,000 buried "under the big dubbya."

Unable to agree on how to divide the loot once it's found, the motorists carefully and calculatingly embark independently. The race is on. The greedy group of motorists who compete for the lead are: a pair of madcap buddies (Mickey Rooney and Buddy Hackett); a henpecked husband (Milton Berle) and his wife (Dorothy Provine) and raucous mother-in-law (Ethel Merman); a dentist and his wife on their second honeymoon (Sid Caesar and Edie Adams); and a truck driver (Jonathan Winters).

As the group of lunatics race toward the mysterious destination, they are unknowingly followed by the police in squad cars and helicopters, monitoring their every move. The lead detective on the case (Spencer Tracy) has his own plan in mind: to abscond with the loot once it's been discovered.

The wild and maniacal chase down the coast of Southern California includes hysterical disasters, close calls, explosions, and an accumulation of more interested treasure hunters along the way. In the end . . . no one wins the lottery.

Sidelights

- Touted as a motion picture that included every major comedian working in those days, the film actually lacked a slew of major personalities that one might expect in an extravaganza such this: Bob Hope, Lucille Ball, Red Skelton, Jackie Gleason, Groucho Marx, Art Carney, Phyllis Diller, and Dick Van Dyke, just to name a few.

- As far as budget and sheer star-studded scope of projects go, *Mad World* remains the most significant production to feature the name and work of Don Knotts. In the film, Don portrays an unwilling driver for Phil Silvers, who suddenly commandeers the "Nervous Man's" vehicle, barking orders at him. The scenes display Knotts at his scattered best. And yet, in his autobiography, he strangely offers just a passing mention of the epic motion picture. Granted, in *Mad World* his role is brief—but memorable—and it probably meant just two days' work for him (and a paycheck that reflected such). So, in that arena Knotts virtually paid no attention to the classic film as it compared to the rest of his body of work. Maybe he was unhappy that some of his scenes were sliced out of the film?

- While many critics at the time complained that the movie should be trimmed, that's exactly what the studio did—which infuriated director Stanley Kramer. When the film premiered, it ran 195 minutes. When the studio took scissors to Kramer's masterpiece a few weeks later, moviegoers around the country saw a different picture, this one trimmed and running 154 minutes. The studio cut not only the existing prints they had on hand, but also the film's original negative. To this day, the complete motion picture, in its intended entirety, has not been found. In 2001, several film collectors undertook a massive scavenger hunt to locate the missing footage—a search that yielded a few minutes of the missing video and sound elements. The missing thirty-five minutes of footage have yet to be found. Excised from the original print are scenes involving Spencer Tracey and Buster Keaton, Sid Caesar and Edie Adams, as well as Don Knotts and Barbara Pepper. The cut scenes with Don Knotts are verified by existing photography taken during the production.

The scene involving Knotts (in the script he's identified as "Very Nervous Man") and Barbara Pepper takes place after conniving Otto Meyer (Phil Silvers) hops in Knotts's car. They are being followed by a helicopter. Silvers frantically instructs Knotts to locate a telephone and make an emergency call to authorities in Washington, D.C. Knotts, in hilarious desperation, pulls in at a small-town drugstore, and Scene 329, as it appears in the second draft of the shooting script, takes place:

329. EXTERIOR OUTSIDE SMALL TOWN DRUGSTORE
The Very Nervous Man, who has tried to interrupt these exhortations several times, now flings another panic-stricken glance at the helicopter and runs into the drugstore. Through the plate glass window, we can see him as he runs up to two telephone booths, both of which are occupied, inside. At about that point, Otto Meyer shifts over in the seat and, permitting himself a small smile, drives away off-screen. Inside the drugstore, the Very Nervous Man makes an effort to get the people who are talking on the two phones to let him interrupt. They refuse. He appears to be shouting at them. Then, as he attempts to take the receiver out of the hand of a Large Irate Lady in one of the booths, she offers some stout resistance. The business builds up until there is a considerable commotion. The shot might hold until the Very Nervous Man, who is now obviously hysterical, has been placed under physical restraint.

• Screenwriter/critic/blogger Mark Evanier (povonline.com) makes some astute points about the film and Don Knotts's time on-screen. Following his attendance at an anniversary screening of the film at a packed Los Angeles theater, Evanier commented:

It's a Mad, Mad, Mad, Mad World is probably my favorite movie. I don't think it's the best movie I've ever seen. I don't even think it's the funniest. But, like a piece of art that grabs your eye and won't let go, I find it fascinating. . . .

One of the interesting things about this movie is that a certain amount of its humor flows from having some knowledge of the actors involved. For example, there's a scene where Phil Silvers—cast in his eternal role as an avaricious con artist—is in desperate need of a ride somewhere, lest he lose out on his shot at the $350,000 everyone is chasing after. (I'm assuming here you already know the plot. If not, basically, it's that that amount of money is buried somewhere and one person after another gets caught up in mad pursuit of it.)

So Silvers flags down a car and as it pulls up, we see that its driver is Don Knotts. Enormous laugh. Even before anything is said or done to Mr. Knotts by Mr. Silvers, the audience is laughing . . . because they know that Phil Silvers is a predator and Don Knotts is prey, and the matchup just seems so perfect as to be funny. It's like a joke where the setup is so good, you're chuckling long before you get anywhere near the punch line. *Mad World* is full of such moments in which the audience is one notch ahead of the film.

Tonight, some in the house knew the film so well, we were two notches ahead. In the above scene, we were laughing before we even saw that the driver was Don Knotts. We all knew it would be Don Knotts because we all knew the movie. So we laughed before we saw Don and, when we finally did, we applauded him. Matter of fact, most of those present applauded the first on-screen appearance of each great comedian and character actor, which meant a lot of applause.

- Veteran *Mad* magazine artist Jack Davis created the phenomenal caricature artwork for the film's publicity campaign as well as the artwork for the cover of the *Mad* paperback, *It's a World, World, World, World Mad,* where he spoofed his own artwork.
- Veteran comedian Joe Besser (at one time a member of the Three Stooges) was approached by Stanley Kramer to play one of the gas station attendants who does combat with Jonathan Winters. Besser was disappointed because he was forced to decline due to his contract as a regular on ABC-TV's sitcom *The Joey Bishop Show.* It's too bad, since that scene—eventually coming to pass with the hilarious talents of Arnold Stang and Marvin Kaplan—ended up one of the more glorious moments in the film. Arnold Stang broke his wrist the day before shooting the highly manic gas station scene and concealed the bulky cast by wearing a large glove.

Behind the Scenes

It's a Mad, Mad, Mad, Mad World premiered on November 7, 1963, at Hollywood's brand-new Cinerama Theatre. The $9.4 million movie was produced, from conception to release, in three and a half years. Producer Stanley Kramer took 166 shooting days, over the period of seven and a half months, to actually film the lengthy screenplay. In the process, Kramer exposed 636,000 feet of Technicolor film (approximately 125 miles). A total of thirty-four professional film stuntmen were utilized in capturing the extensive chaotic scenes. The special-effects artists and technicians worked overtime accomplishing a fantastic array of breathtaking explosions, crashes, fires, breakaway buildings, dust clouds, sparks—you name it.

The film was shot in 70-millimeter Ultra Panavision for viewing exclusively at Cinerama theaters across the country. Cinerama theaters had screens that were almost half round and seemed to envelop the audience. Up to that point, the Cinerama effect was achieved with the use of combining three projectors and three images lined up on-screen. With the development of the new seamless single-lens projection system, the giant Cinerama picture was blended perfectly, retaining the giant image. To further enhance the scope of this undertaking, Stanley Kramer hired the entire ninety-seven-member Los Angeles Philharmonic Orchestra, led by Ernest Gold, composer of the movie's score. Gold went on to win an Academy Award for the movie's final theme, called "Exodus." The explosive epic was nominated for six Academy Awards and took home two—in sound effects and music. The film pulled in $20.8 million in initial box-office revenue.

Reviews

The New York Times: "A wonderfully crazy and colorful 'chase' comedy!"

Chicago Tribune: "If you have a hearty appetite for slapstick, this may be for you. . . . Mack Sennett, who originated this type of burlesque of the detective drama by stressing visual humor, wisely kept his offerings brief. Fun is fun, but one must know when to quit. Quick, Mr. Kramer, the scissors!"

Los Angeles Herald-Examiner: "*It's a Mad, Mad, Mad, Mad World* has more belly-laughs than any other comedy in the history of the screen. . . . It ought to have. Stanley Kramer's slapstick extravaganza . . . is three hours and 30 minutes long, including intermission. . . . It is too, too much for its own good."

TV Guide: "Overkill, the *Cleopatra* of the funny-bone. This comic extravaganza starts off funny, but exhausts rather than delights. Designed to be the biggest, most lavish comedy ever made, *It's a Mad, Mad, Mad, Mad World* is a coarse, star-studded pageant of Keystone Kops–style slapstick."

Newsweek: "bad, bad, bad, bad . . . It is redundant, ridiculous, and too insistent . . . the title writer just didn't know when to stop; neither did the moviemaker Stanley Kramer. . . . At the end of the long, long, long, long film one leaves in about as good a humor as a highway patrolman after a bad day on the freeway."

MOVE OVER, DARLING

Released: 1963
Produced by: Martin Melcher, Aaron Rosenberg
Written by: Bella Spewack, Sam Spewack, Leo McCarey
Screenplay by: Hal Kanter and Jack Sher
Directed by: Michael Gordon
Running Time: 103 minutes
20th Century Fox

Cast

Doris Day (Ellen Wagstaff Arden), James Garner (Nicholas Arden), Polly Bergen (Bianca Steele), Thelma Ritter (Grace Arden), Fred Clark (Mr. Codd), Don Knotts (Shoe Salesman), Elliot Reid (Dr. Herman Schlick), Edgar Buchanan (Judge Bryson), John Astin (Clyde Prokey), Pat Harrington Jr. (District Attorney), Eddie Quillan (Bellboy), Max Showalter (Hotel Desk Clerk), Alvy Moore (Room Service Waiter), Pami Lee (Jenny Arden), Leslie Farrell (Didi Arden), Chuck Conners (Stephen "Adam" Burkett), Jimmy Bays (Doorman), Joel Collins (Ambulance Attendant), Christopher Connelly (Ranking Seaman), Bing Davidson (Ensign J.G.), Mel Flory (Seaman), Bess Flowers (Seymour's Wife), Kelton Garwood (Ambulance Attendant), Mary George (Hotel Maid), Herold Goodwin (Bailiff), Sid Gould (Waiter at Pool), Billy Halop (Seaman), John Harmon (Taxi Driver), Ted Jacques (Pool Attendant), Edward McNally (Commander), Joseph Mell (Stock Clerk), Emile Meyer (Process Server), Pat Moran (Seymour), Jack Orrison (Bartender), James Patridge (Skipper), Stan Richards (Officer), Sheila Rogers (Secretary), Michael Romanoff (Floorwalker), Rachel Romen (Injured Man's Wife), Jack Sahakian (Executive Officer J.G.), Alan Sues (Court

Don and Doris Day on the set of *Move Over, Darling*.

Clerk), Brad Trumble (Process Server), Rosa Turich (Maria), Mike McLean (Bellboy), Jean Blackford (Woman), Peter Walker (PIO Officer), Richard Collier (Cabdriver), Karen Norris (Saleswoman), Mark Bailey (Assistant Stock Clerk)

Synopsis

Nick Arden is about to be married . . . only there's one problem. He must go before a judge to have his long-missing first wife, Ellen, declared legally dead after five years. Unbeknownst to Nick, his wife has been rescued from a desert island. Landing in San Pedro, Ellen is unable to phone home, so she heads directly to her old residence, there finding her children, who don't even recognize her. Heartbroken, she decides not to tell them she is their long-lost mother. Finally, she hears the news of her husband's plans to remarry from her shocked mother-in-law. She is desperate once she also learns that he is about to be remarried that very day!

With no time to waste, Ellen proceeds to the honeymoon hotel in order to reclaim her husband. Nick arrives at the hotel with his new bride, Bianca, and is stunned to find his first wife alive and well. Ellen insists that Nick reveal to Bianca that she is alive and she wants her husband back. Garner desperately shuttles his two wives between two hotel rooms and fakes a back injury, all the while frantically trying to figure out what to do next. He is torn between the two ladies in his life and doesn't want to hurt either one of them. Meanwhile, he accidentally learns that Ellen has spent the five years on the island with another man and becomes jealous. After more mix-ups, Bianca walks out on Nick, allowing him to be reunited with Ellen.

Sidelights/Behind the Scenes

- The film was completed July 16, 1963, for a Christmas Day release that year.
- In 1962, the news had hit that Marilyn Monroe would be teamed with singer/actor Dean Martin for a new film comedy titled *Something's Got to Give* produced by 20th Century Fox, with a script written by Nunnally Johnson. It was to be a comeback comedy for the blonde bombshell. The film was a remake of the 1940 screwball comedy film *My Favorite Wife,* starring Irene Dunne, Cary Grant, and Randolph Scott. *Something's Got to Give* was cast and production was under way by early June 1962; however, the production was in crisis just two weeks into shooting. Marilyn Monroe, claiming illnesses, reported to work only one day in the first fifteen days of shooting. Director George Cukor shot around her with scenes involving costars Dean Mar-

tin, Cyd Charisse, and Wally Cox, but eventually he could continue no more.

Producer Henry Weinstein told the *Los Angeles Herald-Examiner* in an interview on July 6 that a crisis had been reached and decisions would have to be made. Weinstein said: "There has had to be an agonizing reappraisal of the situation. . . . We have to decide whether Marilyn can recover in time to continue with the production, and if the studio can stand further delays. We certainly want her to continue. I think she really is sick. I believe she wanted to do this picture and has the highest regards for it. But if her absence continues, the studio simply has to make a decision." Just two days later, Monroe was officially dropped from the film and the entire production was suspended and eventually shelved. (Monroe died two months later, on August 5, 1962, at the age of thirty-six.)

One year later, the script and production team for *Something's Got to Give* had been completely overhauled, and the newly renovated picture, *Move Over, Darling,* was recast with starring roles played by Doris Day and James Garner.

- Due to the problematic delays and suspension and release of Marilyn Monroe, costar Dean Martin decided to protest and informed 20th Century Fox that he would not continue in the film if Monroe did not return. The studio filed a $3.3 million damage suit against the singer. Martin countersued the studio for $6.8 million in damages. One year later, all lawsuits were dropped, according to *Variety.*
- Don Knotts replaced comic actor Wally Cox when the film was recast. Producers Marty Melcher and Aaron Rosenberg said at the time that this was the only scene they had decided not to alter from the way it was shot previously with the late Marilyn Monroe and Wally Cox.
- In Doris Day's carwash scene, shot on the final day of the production, the actress broke a rib.

Reviews

The New Yorker: "There are movie properties that, under one title or another, are doomed to be made over and over, sometimes well and sometimes badly; *Move Over, Darling* is such a property, and maybe next time it will turn out fine."

Films & Filming: "Certainly the best of Doris Day's recent comedies, *Move Over, Darling* is generally a chucklesome affair. . . . Anyone looking for a chunk of high-style Hollywood sophistication is likely to be disappointed; but anyone in the market for a piece of chromium-plated foolishness is bound to enjoy it."

Saturday Review: "Unfortunately, the suspense immediately is lost, because it would be inconceivable in the Hollywood scheme of things to have the country's No. 1 box office star lose her husband to Polly Bergen (who was unranked in the last exhibitor's poll) and, besides, Miss Bergen is made to play such a harsh-voiced, domineering wretch that almost anyone, including a long-lost wife, would be preferable."

Variety: "When *Move Over, Darling* relies for the most part on the inspiration of the past, it delivers comedy that is ageless and universal in appeal. When it breaks anchor and drifts from its moorings, the reconstructed vessel winds up in turbulent, uncharted waters and starts to flounder."

Los Angeles Herald-Examiner: "Doris Day and Don Knotts (a standout on the *Andy Griffith* TV show) have all the ingredients for one of the funniest sequences in *Move Over, Darling*. The actress seduces the comedian, who plays a Casper Milquetoast type shoe clerk."

THE INCREDIBLE MR. LIMPET

Released: 1964
Produced by: John C. Rose
Written by: Jameson Brewer, Joe DiMona, John C. Rose, Theodore Pratt (Novel)
Directed by: Arthur Lubin
Animation Sequences Directed by: Vladimir "Bill" Tytla
Running Time: 99 minutes
Warner Bros.

Cast

Don Knotts (Henry Limpet), Carole Cook (Bessie Limpet), Jack Weston (George Stickel, USN), Andrew Duggan (Cmdr. Robert L. Harlock, USN), Larry Keating (Adm. Perry P. Spewter, USN), Oscar Beregi Jr. (Admiral Doemitz), Charles Meredith (Fleet Admiral Fivestar, USN), Elizabeth MacRae (Voice of Lady Fish), Paul Frees (Voice of Crusty), Jack Pepper, Phil Arnold (Fishermen), Cordy Clarke (Giggling Girl), Lisabeth Field (Miss Barnes), John Truax (Policeman), Peter Adams (Lieutenant), Logan Field (Lieutenant J.G.), Monte Plyler (Helmsman), Royden Clark, Jack Shea, Al Checco, Henry Norell, John Hale (Sailors), Walter Friedel (Nazi Officer), Felix Reinsch (Sub Captain), Heinz Sadler, Paul Busch (Sonar Men), Harold Dyrenforth (U-Boat Captain), Feridun Colgecen, Edward Wermel (Scientists)

Synopsis

Nebbish Henry Limpet, a mild-mannered Brooklyn bookkeeper, irritates his wife, Bessie, because of his great love for fish. He has such a strong attraction to aquatic life, that he actually yearns to become a fish . . . he even sings about it. It's World War II, and Limpet's attempt to join the navy fails

Bessie Limpet (Carole Cook) kisses her husband good-bye in *The Incredible Mr. Limpet.*

because he is 4-F due to poor eyesight. Matters are made worse when his best friend, George Stickle, is accepted into the navy and shipped out. One day Henry, Bessie, and George (who has returned on leave)

ABOVE: Bessie Limpet demands that Henry cease the fishy nonsense. RIGHT: Henry Limpet always dreamed of enlisting in the service.

THE INCREDIBLE MR. DON KNOTTS

visit Coney Island for a fun afternoon near the ocean. Henry accidentally falls off a dock, disappears into the ocean, and is miraculously transformed into a fish. Content with the transformation, he makes underwater friends with a sea crustacean and falls in love with a female fish he names "Lady Fish." With the outbreak of World War II, Limpet finally helps the war cause and guides the U.S. sub chasers in tracking and sinking German U-boats. Although baffled by their success, the navy bestows a commission upon fishy Limpet. At the war's conclusion, he surfaces for a poignant farewell to his wife and swims off with Lady Fish.

Sidelights

- Filming was completed on July 26, 1962.
- Don Knotts sings for the first time on film, a terrific little song called "I Wish I Were a Fish"—really a highlight of the film. Singer and TV/radio personality Arthur Godfrey recorded the song for release on a 45 rpm, which was available when the film debuted.
- Director Arthur Lubin had a great experience with this type of suspended belief in film and television. Lubin not only directed some of Universal Studios' Francis the Talking Mule movies, but he also directed and produced episodes of TV's *Mr. Ed* (the talking horse, of course, of course).
- *The Incredible Mr. Limpet* spawned a 12-cent Dell comic book featuring Don Knotts on the cover as Adm. Henry Limpet. Dell printed 350,000 copies of the special movie-edition comic book. Today, in mint condition, the comic sells for more than $100.
- The movie premiered January 17, 1964, at Weeki Wachee, Florida, during a mega-publicity blitz and press junket orchestrated by Warner Bros. The Los Angeles premiere was held at the Palace Theater on March 18, 1964.

    The Weeki Wachee event, located near Brooksville on Florida's west coast, was touted as the world's first underwater premiere—the first "dive-in" theater, you might say. More than two hundred members of the press were flown in for this three-day junket and invited to watch the film in a special five-hundred-seat the-

The *pince nez* eyeglasses worn by Don Knotts in *Limpet* were originally used by actor Paul Muni in the 1935 film *The Story of Louis Pasteur.* The studio prop department fit Knotts specifically with this eyewear for the film.

Fish Out of Water Henry Limpet longs to join the sea world.

ABOVE AND LEFT: The cast joins Arthur Godfrey for some promotional chores in Florida during the premiere events for *The Incredible Mr. Limpet.*

ater sixteen feet below the surface, where mermaids performed underwater. The screen on which Limpet was projected was twenty feet under the crystal clear waters of the spring. The theater featured nineteen huge plate-glass windows, each two and a half inches thick, which allowed for viewing. Members of the press were given exclusive access to the film's stars for interviews during the tour. The shapely Weeki Wachee performing mermaids were hostesses during the event.

- The animation was handled by the competent artists and painters of the Warner Brothers animation department—long known for the creation of such legendary cartoon characters as Bugs Bunny, Daffy Duck, and Porky Pig. *Variety* pointed out in 1964: "Producer John Rose is a former longtime production associate of Walt Disney's and his work herein is mightily suggestive of Disney." One of the assistant animators to work on *Limpet* was Phil Roman, a veteran who in 1984 founded the award-winning independent animation studio known as Film Roman—which has since produced the animation for TV's *The Simpsons, King of the Hill,* and *Garfield.* Additional veteran Warner Bros. animators who worked on scenes were: Gerry Chiniquy, Hawley Pratt, Robert McKimson, Maurice Noble, and Don Peters.
- One of the earlier titles considered for the film was *Be Careful How You Wish.* The film's story was developed from a novel titled *Mr. Limpet* by Florida writer Theodore Pratt.
- In the "hero" montage, Henry Limpet (as the smiling fish) is imagined to be on the cover of *Life* magazine, the center of a

ticker-tape parade. *Life* prepared the artwork for the brief sight gag and eventually ran the faux cover image in a feature spread in their own pages.

- Legendary voice-over actor Paul Frees supplied the voice of Crusty the Hermit Crab. Some may recall Frees's vocals as the bombastic "Burger Meister Meister Burger" in the perennial Rankin/Bass stop-motion Christmas TV special, *Santa Claus Is Coming to Town.* Frees recorded much dialogue for Walt Disney's attractions in Disneyland, such as narration in the Haunted Mansion.

- Accomplished songwriters Sammy Fain and Harold Adamson were teamed for the first time for Limpet. Fain, who had hits with "By the Waterfall" and "Love Is a Many-Splendored Thing," worked closely with Adamson, who wrote the lyrics for the film *Around the World in 80 Days,* to create five new tunes for Limpet.

- Despite a publicity blitz that attracted press, both print and television, from all corners of the nation, *Limpet* did merely adequate business at the box office, certainly disappointing the studio and the star himself. Said Don Knotts years later: "I don't think the powers that be at the studio quite understood the picture. According to the director, Arthur Lubin, Jack Warner, who had been watching the dailies, sent him a memo one day that read: 'You've got a funny actor down there. Why don't you give him something funny to do?' *Mr. Limpet* was not supposed to be funny. Quaint and amusing, yes, but not funny. I thought it turned out to be a splendid motion picture. They had been working hard to get the picture into the Radio City Music Hall in New York . . . for an Easter release. The story I heard was that they decided against it because the name Don Knotts did not have a motion-picture track record."

- When Limpet was released, Don Knotts landed on the cover of *Tropical Fish Hobbyist* magazine (April 1964), a publication for fish lovers that swims and surfaces in magazine racks still today. The article inside the issue noted that *Limpet* was a tremendous boost for the hobby, as described by the NAPI (National Association of the Pet Industry).

Behind the Scenes

- In order for the animators to closely parody Don Knotts's face, they had the actor sit for a series of photography sessions. The artists were able to turn flesh to fish in creating a fantastic animated likeness of Knotts as a fish, complete with distinctive facial features.

- All of the aquatic scenes—including the Coney Island pier and the naval scenes—were filmed on Warner Brothers Studio's famed Stage 16. The massive soundstage, built in the early 1930s, includes a tank that holds two and a half million gallons of water. Stage 16 is currently the largest soundstage in Hollywood, with a ceiling reaching ninety-eight feet. Additional films shot on Stage 16 over the decades (some utilizing the tank, others the main flooring) include: *Casablanca, My Fair Lady, The Music Man, Annie, The Big Sleep, The Great Race, The Poseidon Adventure, The Perfect Storm,* and *Indiana Jones and the Kingdom of the Crystal Skull.*
- The *Limpet* cast and crew spent a week on location at the Long Beach, California, naval base, filming aboard and around the destroyer *USS Maddox,* which saw heavy action in World War II and during the Korean conflict.
- *Sounds Fishy. . . .* According to the Warner Brothers press book for the film, a scene involving Henry Limpet's fish tank full of colorful beauties had to be quickly reshot because of a tragic mistake: "When the time came to shoot the scene, it was found that all the fish except one were devoured or dead. Through an oversight by the prop department, a lethal South American piranha had been put into the tank, too. That part of the collection not yet eaten by the piranha had been frightened to death."

Reviews

Life: "*The Incredible Mr. Limpet* is a fine, funny fish story that skillfully blends cartoons and live action. With his watery eyes, rubbery mouth, and anxious dorsal movements, Don Knotts, deputy sheriff of the *Andy Griffith* television show, is perfectly cast as Mr. Limpet. The kids will be delighted with the Warner Brothers fantasy, and many more sophisticated grownups may envy Henry Limpet as the one that got away."

Variety: "The film itself, if far out in nuttiness, theme-wise, has to do with a man who wishes so hard to become a fish he indeed turns into a fish. . . . An imaginative cinematic outing that has got to be at least agreeable, and then there's the possibility it might register so soundly as to become particularly meaningful commercially."

Hollywood Reporter: "*The Incredible Mr. Limpet* is a charming, funny film, a novelty comedy in live action and animation with songs. It is getting a heavy exploitation sendoff and combined with its basic values this should make it a good box office attraction."

Boxoffice: "A completely offbeat comedy that combines live action and animated cartoon techniques, along with the wildest fantasy that ever hit the screen . . . a most unusual picture."

Interview: Carole Cook

You were known as a musical comedy actress, onstage mostly. . . . Had you done films before Mr. Limpet?

It was my first movie. The excitement was tremendous. I remember I auditioned for it. I had been out here in California a short time. Lucille Ball brought me out here.

I remember very well going to Warner Bros. and I remember reading for John Rose, the producer, and Arthur Lubin, the director. We met in the office and I read for them.

Up until that time, I had not met Don until the first day of rehearsal. When I read the script I remember thinking how right it was for him, just perfect for him, from what I knew of his talents.

What scenes do you vividly remember from Limpet?

Our very first scene was on the subway where I'm wearing a big hat. Both Jack Weston and Don were extremely nice to me because I came from the theater. When they said, "Hit your mark," I had no idea what that meant. They were protective of me.

My favorite scene was where I'm on the pier and I talk to the fish when he's leaving and I put glasses on him. It was a sweet scene. I loved it because it was so real. I remember I had to talk to a red ball that was in the water and they later erased the red ball and put in the fish with the animation. We were in the famous tank on the Warner lot, this mammoth stage tank with

water. It was all indoors. They'd used that stage for all kinds of shipwreck movies and famous movies with ships and ocean scenes.

And Don volunteered—as a lot of big stars who are worth their salt do—to do the voice at the side during the scene. They could have just had the assistant director say the lines, but Don said , "No, I want to do my voice." Don was ten feet away from me on something like a ramp out in the water so he could lean down. It was difficult for me to talk to a red ball when his voice was to my right somewhere and my tendency was to want to look at him, but it worked out. They kept saying, "This is not the theater . . . talk to the red ball." They had a close-up on me and I had a tear in my eye. I loved that quiet scene. Don came up to me later and said, "You broke my heart, Carole, you broke my heart." I thought that was so sweet of him. It was easier to do that scene with him there.

Don was generous that way and he stayed that afternoon. I thought that was sweet of him; I've always remembered that. He was always there for my close-ups and he was always there to do the exchange with me even though he was off-camera.

Do you know who originally recorded Lady Fish?

I did! When they were looking for the voice of Lady Fish, they had me do it at one time. I went into a recording studio and they thought it might be interesting as a subliminal thing for Lady Fish to have some of the qualities of Bessie's voice. They asked me to alter my voice and had me "make her lighter and dreamlike."

I made my voice much softer and kind of southern. I remember that Don was happy with the way it turned out. Don was supportive and always for me, you know, but in the end they used an actress named Elizabeth MacRae.

When I think about it, I wasn't really disappointed that they'd replaced me. After all, I was Bessie Limpet, so what did I care? They were trying a lot of different things. I don't know if they auditioned anyone else.

Was Andy Griffith on the set with Don at all?

Yes, I remember Andy Griffith would come on the set to see Don, and I'm telling you, that was one of my favorite memories because the two of them together, on a personal note, they would go into routines out of nowhere and assume characters or personalities . . . like two WWII veterans talking or something like that. They were hysterical together. Just off the cuff improvising for the people around them. That was something they were used to doing. Or next they'd be two zookeepers and go into a routine. One time they did a routine, and Andy Griffith talked for about fifteen minutes and he played like he was in some big convention hall and it was a convention of sex therapists and he would say, "Now we've got a wonderful speaker today. Some of the language will be very technical and clinical because we're talking about sexual things. . . . And now we have Dr. Don Knotts." Then Don looked up and said some of the saltiest things. . . . He did it in that quivering voice of his. Well, I nearly died. Isn't that funny?

OPPOSITE: This rare behind the scenes candid was taken in between takes of filming *Limpet*. Notice the cigarette in Jack Weston's hand.

A Few Words from Elizabeth MacRae, aka "Lady Fish"

You'd never believe it, but I didn't meet Don until early 1964 down in Weeki Wachi Springs for the press junket for *Mr. Limpet*. That was two years after we had made the film. I never actually worked with Don during the film.

Don had done his role and there was another actress who voiced the Lady Fish, and it didn't work out. I think they wanted a little bit more of a seductress type, softer type for Lady Fish. They had done their scenes together and recorded them. I got a call from an agent and they said they wanted to rerecord the Lady Fish character.

I went to Warner Brothers and met Arthur Lubin and went into a recording room, like a dubbing studio, and the stage manager read the Don Knotts part. They told me a little bit about the character. It just happened. It was kind of magical, and I became Lady Fish. I did my whole part in less than an hour. Then they drew the characters, the fish looked just like him—and they made Lady Fish look like me. They were working from photographs.

Don was absolutely brilliant in the film. He became the fish. Our chemistry worked very well. You had to believe that Don's character would leave his human wife not only for his life under the sea, but also because he was in love with Lady Fish. You had to believe that she was innocent and a virgin fish. Remember, she kept inviting him to go to the spawning ground.

It was a big breakthrough movie because it was the first time Warner Brothers had joined the animation with the live action and it caught on. I've had more people mention that film, even though you never see me, but because of my voice. It was not unlike the character Lou Ann Poovie on *Gomer Pyle*.

THE GHOST AND MR. CHICKEN

Released: 1966
Produced by: Edward J. Montagne
Written by: Jim Fritzell, Everett Greenbaum
Directed by: Alan Rafkin
Running Time: 90 minutes
Universal Studios

Cast

Don Knotts (Luther Heggs), Joan Staley (Alma Parker), Liam Redmond (Kelsey), Dick Sargent (George Beckett), Skip Homeier (Ollie Weaver), Reta Shaw (Mrs. Halcyon Maxwell), Lurene Tuttle (Mrs. Natalie Miller), Phil Ober (Nicholas Simmons), Harry Hickox (Police Chief Art Fuller), Charles Lane (Mr. Whitlow), Jesslyn Fax (Mrs. Hutchinson), Nydia Westman (Mrs. Cobb), George Chandler (Judge Harley Nast), Robert Cornthwaite (Springer), Jim Begg (Herkie), Sandra Gould (Loretta Pine), James Millhollin (Mr. Milo Maxwell), Cliff Norton (Charlie, the Bailiff), Ellen Corby (Miss Neva Tremaine), Jim Boles (Billy Ray Fox), Phil Arnold (Jury Foreman), Ceil Cabot (Occult Society Clubwoman), Al Checco (Gaylord Patie), Herbie Faye (Man in Diner), Everett Greenbaum ("Attaboy, Luther" Voice), Harry Hines (Bum at Picnic), Bern Hoffman (J. T. Barringer, Heavy Policeman at Station), Florence Lake (Occult Society Clubwoman), Dorothy Love (Occult Society Clubwoman), J. Edward McKinley (Mayor Carlyle Preston), Burt Mustin (Mr. Deligondo), Eddie Quillan (Elevator Operator), Hal Smith (Calver Weems), Hope Summers (Suzanna Blush), Ruth Thom (Occult Society Clubwoman), Dick Wilson (Band Leader), Maxine Semon (Occult Society Clubwoman), Margaret Wheeler (Occult Society Clubwoman), Dorothy Keller (Occult Society Clubwoman), Billie Frederick (Woman Juror), Lilian Field (Edna June Weems), Lee Krieger (Charlie, Process Server), Joan Granville (Waitress), Adair Jameson (Eileen), Ella Edwards (Cashier),

> "Calm? Calm? Do murder and calm go together? Calm and murder? *Murder!*"
>
> —LUTHER HEGGS

"It was a board that thick!"

NEXT PAGE: Luther whips his Edsel around.

Teddy Quinn (Autograph Kid), Ralph Montgomery (Man at Mailbox), Gerry Lock (Adlib Woman), Rand Barker (Adlib Man), Ralph Neff (Adlib Man), Roy Johnson (Adlib #1), Jack Carol (Adlib #2), Florence Ravenel (Adlib #3), Jimmy Bracken (Running Kid Picnic), Kim Slevin (Norma Jean Wexler), Stig Eldred (Billy Wexler)

Synopsis

In the quaint town of Rachel, Kansas, the stately old Simmons mansion, a Victorian beauty in its day, has fallen into disrepair and been ordered to be demolished by its owner, Nicholas Simmons. According to the town's legend it was a "murder house" twenty years earlier, when a man killed his wife then jumped from the tower to his death. As the story goes, you can hear the ghost of Mr. Simmons playing the haunting organ at midnight.

Luther Heggs, a cub reporter for the *Rachel Courier Express,* assumes he has stumbled upon a murder scene right in front of the mansion while driving home one night. In order to exploit the mansion's imminent destruction, Luther is assigned to spend a night in the "murder house" (murder "and suicide" as some townsfolk point out) on the night of the twentieth anniversary of the murders. At midnight, a frazzled Luther witnesses the old organ playing by itself, a secret passageway opening, and a series of maniacal events that send him fleeing the house before morning. The following day, the story is published of his eerie experiences in the mansion, and it sets the town abuzz. Even the banker's wife, a spiritualist, refuses to allow the house to be destroyed, claiming it to be a center of spiritualistic revelation.

Nicholas Simmons, nephew of the deceased couple, takes Luther Heggs to court, alleging his family name has been publicly smeared. While Heggs becomes the town hero and delivers a bizarre speech at a park luncheon, he is also summoned to a trial. In court, Heggs is interrogated and made

ABOVE: Chicken noodle soup with Alma. BELOW: "It was terrible, just terrible.... I'll never get over it as long as I live."

The Ghost and Mr. Chicken house in the film and as it looks today, on the Universal Studios backlot, remodeled and manicured. More recently, the structure has been used for the television show *Desperate Housewives.*

to look ridiculous by not only his own responses but those of witnesses called in the process, such as his grade school teacher. The judge orders the jury to the Simmons house at midnight to investigate Heggs's claims. Of course, nothing out of the ordinary occurs and everyone leaves disappointed and distrustful of Heggs. Meanwhile, after everyone has vacated the premises, Heggs witnesses the old organ playing and discovers it was Mr. Kelsey, the newspaper's janitor, pounding the keys. Heggs and Kelsey confront Nicholas Simmons in the house and determine that he was the one who killed his uncle and aunt years ago in the mansion. In desperation, Simmons has taken a hostage and it's up to Heggs to save lovely Alma Parker, his girlfriend, from harm. Luther delivers an awkward karate maneuver to the backside of Nicholas Simmons, saving Alma, and soon the case is closed. In the end, Luther marries Alma and the wedding includes some eerie surprises.

Sidelights

- Filming was completed on July 29, 1965.
- Andy Griffith collaborated with the writers on the script, but went uncredited.
- The original title of this film was *Running Scared*. Disney Studios called the writers, Everett Greenbaum and Jim Fritzell, and requested to utilize the title for something that was active at their studio. "So we let them," Greenbaum said. "They didn't do anything with it until many years later with Billy Crystal."
- *Chicken Nugget:* Cut from the movie's Sunday picnic scene are shots of a big dog running up and jumping on Luther Heggs and knocking him flat on the ground. The movie's press book reveals that it took the tactic of the animal trainer (one of the famous Weatherwax family) smearing ground beef on Knotts's face to provoke the dog to lick him unmercifully.
- Don Knotts's stuntman for this film was Jerry Brutsche, who was also busy doing stunts and falls at the time for Irene "Granny" Ryan on TV's *The Beverly Hillbillies.* His masterful Luther

Inside the spooky Simmons mansion, Luther nearly messes his pants as he encounters the spiritual surprises, including the bloodstained organ keys (". . . and they used Bon Ami!").

Heggs's flip forward into an elevator is something Brutsche was especially proud of in this film.

- The house used as the Simmons mansion on Universal Studios' Colonial Street back lot was used as Jimmy Stewart's residence in the film *Harvey* (1950). It has since been modified and is currently used prominently in the TV series *Desperate Housewives.* Next door: The Munsters' mansion (aka 1313 Mockingbird Lane). Across the street: June and Ward Cleaver's house.
- The running gag-line "Attaboy, Luther!" was yelled out by screenwriter Everett Greenbaum. "I had the idea for the town heckler and I yelled it as we were writing it," said Greenbaum. "Then when we were gonna shoot it, Alan Rafkin, the director, wanted to do it. Well, he didn't do it right. So I went in and recorded a series of 'attaboys' at the studio and they added them in postproduction," said Greenbaum.
- The film was released in 1966 as a double feature along with the color film *Munster, Go Home!* starring Fred Gwynne and Yvonne De Carlo.
- *Chickening Out:* After years of fans' demanding this film be released, Universal Studios finally put this and other Knotts features out on home video in 1996.

All Rise Luther and his newspaper, the *Rachel Courier Express,* is sued for libel by Nicholas Simmons.

Good Food The town hero is celebrated at a Chamber of Commerce luncheon.

Filming on Colonial Street on the Universal Studios back lot. In the background you can see the *Chicken* house, and just beyond is the top tier of the *Munsters'* mansion.

- According to the Universal Studios press book for the film: In the opening scenes at the police station, the walls featured "wanted" posters on the giant bulletin board that offered rewards for a variety of criminal types. The photographs on the posters were actually of members of the crew, such as gaffer Les Burnett, grip Paddy Wharfield, and camera operator Bill Dodds.
- Balding actor Phil Ober, who portrayed Mr. Simmons, was married to actress Vivian Vance (Ethel Mertz on *I Love Lucy*) for nearly twenty years.
- *Chicken in Dixie:* Universal Studios was initially uncertain how to market the national release for their low-budget comedy. Don Knotts was not yet an established box-office draw, so they felt they were testing the waters with this film. In Los Angeles, the film opened on April 6, 1966, at the Orpheum Theatre. Prior to the May 1966 national release, the studio decided to try a series of prerelease openings in January in the South: New Orleans, Charlotte (North Carolina), Baton Rouge, Pensacola, Shreveport,

Miami, Dallas, Birmingham (Alabama), among other cities. In some cities, Knotts and his costar Joan Staley made personal appearances. The film did astonishing business and was extended for weeks in nearly every city. *Variety* reported that in Fort Worth, Texas, *Chicken* outsold Rock Hudson's *Man's Favorite Sport* and other popular outings such as *Charade, The Thrill of It All, Shenandoah,* and *To Kill a Mockingbird.*

Bloopers

- Watch that tapioca scene when the banker's wife, Mrs. Maxwell daintily spoons the pudding in. One moment the dessert cup is full, in the next shot it's half empty, then full again.
- When Luther Heggs initially enters the mansion, watch his flashlight. In frantic moments, like his discovery of the organ loft, the beam of light rarely corresponds with the flashlight he's holding.

All Keyed Up Mr. Whitlow (Charles Lane) grills a nerve-racked Luther Heggs on the stand.

Behind the Scenes

Don Knotts is at his spastic best in this movie, one of his most popular. It's filled with Mayberry-isms, as it takes place in a sleepy Mayberry-esque town known as Rachel, Kansas. With many memorable, corny lines, *Ghost* has Knotts scrambling and squawking at his most frantic, all keyed up, just like audiences preferred watching him. This was the pinnacle of scare takes for the actor.

"*The Ghost and Mr. Chicken* is a mother-lode of Mayberry humor," says Ken Beck, coauthor of the best-selling *The Andy Griffith Show Book* and *Aunt Bee's Mayberry Cookbook.* "At least a dozen actors in the movie were regulars or had small but beloved roles on *The Andy Griffith Show.* There are so many little one-line jokes borrowed from the characters in Mayberry, like the line where Luther says he got most of his spunk from his mother."

In its January 1966 review, *The Hollywood Reporter*'s critic made note of another special additive in the film that provided a common bond: "Another thing about the production that is interesting is its use of Negro players. Throughout, in a proportion apparently ratio of the general population, Negroes are seen as part of the general pic-

FOLLOWING PAGES: Judge and jury are off to inspect the Simmons mansion.

ture. If this is a deliberate policy on Universal's part, it is a shrewd move and should be more widely followed. It is probably necessary to add that this does not in any way make this play a racial film. It just gives it a more accurate American flavor."

The movie is commonly thought to have stemmed directly from a haunting *Andy Griffith Show* episode, although the movie's cowriter, Everett Greenbaum, said, "Not really." Greenbaum, a veteran comedy writer and television pioneer, was long partnered with another veteran, Jim Fritzell. These guys invented the television sitcom. Together, they made significant contributions to TV's *Mr. Peepers*, *The Real McCoys*, *The Andy Griffith Show*, and *M*A*S*H*, among others. Greenbaum said in 1996, "We simply knew Don Knotts was greatest when he was scared."

So how did Greenbaum—who grew up in Buffalo—and his partner Fritzell—who hailed from San Francisco—so beautifully capture the unmistakable small-town feel of Mayberry? "Jim and me had an awful lot in common with Andy and Don in regard to comedy and life," Greenbaum admitted. "Even now, when I look at Don or Andy on the screen, I feel like I'm looking in the mirror. It's a very weird feeling. Like I'm them or they're me.

Hal Smith.

"I know Andy's and Don's weaknesses so well; they're both so fragile. Don was so funny—physically—to watch, his wiry body and motions. Hell, Don used to think he was a hunchback in high school."

Many of the film's quirkier, memorable lines—especially from the trial scene—came directly from both writers' childhoods. It was young Fritzell who stumbled around in shoes that were too big because they were his brother's.

"And the skeleton of the squirrel really happened to me," Greenbaum said. "Cal Oaks, this kid I grew up with, and I climbed in this deserted attic in his neighborhood and we found a squirrel skeleton and I've never forgotten it."

And the "Run up an alley and holler fish!" line? "Oh, we used to say that when we were young."

Fritzell and Greenbaum worked on the Universal lot during those years in a bungalow ("right across the road from Cary Grant's bungalow," he said). "We would just laugh all day writing that film," said Greenbaum. "Andy Griffith came in and we all sat around and worked. I laughed so hard they thought I was gonna die. I remember Andy laughed so hard he hit the side of the wall with his fist and it went right through the wall."

Fritzell usually typed while his writing partner bounced around the room acting things out. "There were no lines that one of us wrote alone," Greenbaum pointed out. "It's always a mixture." It was while writing the screenplay for *The Ghost and Mr. Chicken* that Greenbaum and Fritzell shared possibly the most raucous bouts of laughter. And during this time as well, the two of them had maybe one of their most violent disagreements. "It was one of the worst fights I'd ever had with Jim in, oh, thirty years of writing together," Greenbaum revealed.

"Jim wanted the old murder to be done with a gun. I said, 'No! A knife is what an old murder has to be done with! It's much more mysterious.' Jim couldn't understand why the sheers was better, especially when you could show them piercing a painting. I screamed at him until I won," he says, laughing.

And of course, there was a means for the crime. "We were really stopped until Ed Montagne, the producer, said, 'Well, you gotta have a secret stairway.'"

Greenbaum said that Andy Griffith's contributions to the screenplay were valuable and the actor preferred no credit, mainly enjoying the work with his close pal Don Knotts for the fun of it. "I remember Andy saw a screening at the studio and actually fell down laughing at that scene where Don says, 'I prefer good food to bad food any day.' He stole that line and put it in a *Matlock* episode—the same words."

The Hollywood Reporter, in its enthusiastic review, further pointed out: "One of the best things about the Fritzell-Greenbaum script, and Rafkin's direction, is that it stops along the way to create some ancillary comedy. It isn't limited to one joke. There is a scene in a lunchroom, where Knotts has to eat his noodle soup standing up. . . . That sounds frivolous but plays strong."

According to Greenbaum, the

Jim Begg.

Interview with Joan Staley

How were you cast as Don Knotts's costar in The Ghost and Mr. Chicken?

In the business, everything you do counts somewhere. I was in a series called *Broadside* for a brief time; once it was completed and shortly thereafter Ed Montagne at Universal came to me and said, "I have a film for you." I was very honored. Comedy is very difficult, the timing is precise. I was thrilled because it gave me a chance to be out of the dumb blonde type. They told me I would put on a wig. It was right for the character. That was the wig that Claudia Cardinale wore in the movie *Blindfold* with Rock Hudson. It was made for her. It gave a little more something to the image of the all-natural small-town girl.

What scenes were memorable for you?

There were times during rehearsal in the chicken-noodle sequence where I wasn't sure I was going to get through it, Don was so funny, especially with the other guy just sitting there. And then the picnic scene. That wasn't really that pleasant. I really burned my eyes on the reflectors. They had the big reflectors and it was so hot, toward the end of one day. You have to keep your eyes wide open. I did some damage to my eyes. The light for outdoor scenes like that can be very intense. It's like a fireman breathing smoke—not a good thing, but you end up doing it.

Did you watch Don's speech during that scene?

Oh, yes I did. I watched the scene where he goes up and does the speech. I loved it. I was watching a master at work. And you watch and you learn. He was amazing. And we shot it quickly, like television. No wasted time, very quick pace. Really, the movie was so well-planned and easily shot that it was remarkably unremarkable. It was a light set, an easy set, a happy set. Maybe one or two takes for the scenes. And the years of talent added up from all the pros on that set. Everyone in that cast was just a pro.

During the picnic scenes I remember there was a young kid who I just wanted to spank. He was acting up and screwing up takes. His mother was there, but she did nothing. I talked to him, which was not my place, and told him to behave. He was about to get a swat on the bun. Then I saw the director looking at me. Oh, I was upset. The kid was out of control and the mother was just sitting there, saying, "Oh, isn't he such a precious darling?"

Was Don Knotts easy to work with?

Don is really serious about working. He's a very generous spirit. He does not take himself seriously, but he takes his craft very seriously. His basic character was already developed on the Steve Allen "Man on the Street" sketches. One of the nicest to work with and an absolute perfectionist, but he's the type who doesn't impose his perfection on you. He causes you to rise to his level of perfection, which is a beautiful and masterful thing to do. He's an encourager.

How did you approach your character in the film?

Here comes a girl who likes the guy for the guy. Because he was nice. She likes him simply because he's himself. That was the beauty of Rafkin, and Montagne, that team of director and producer. They could take comedy, play the characters for real, border on the farce. It would have been so easy to misdirect it and take it in the wrong areas. It worked. They didn't try to overplay it.

I was working with the great Don Knotts. He put me perfectly at ease. Take the porch scene: First of all, I was scared to death, because it was one of the first scenes we shot. It fit into the schedule that way and required the least number of people, so it was logical. I didn't want Alma to be too inviting, because it would take it in the wrong direction, and not sincere. Timing, sincerity all had to be there. The editing also made it work. That was the crux of the relationship and if that relationship sequence didn't play right, the whole form's gone.

The porch sequence, that was the hardest scene to do. It was complicated, because that's where the characters are made the most bare. As I recall, being totally dependent on the situation, knowing the dialogue, and she's being honest with him. She's not coming on to him, but she's saying, "I'm interested and it's okay for you to be interested." And he's saying, "I want to be. . . ." The scene was about his inner feelings and how did he handle it. That's a very sensitive ground. You don't go tap dancing with cleats on. . . . You're stomping on the squishy parts if you overstep. I didn't want to feel too confident.

Did the fact that you were a Playboy *centerfold (November 1958) cause you to lose any roles at that time or did it help you?*

It probably cost me roles. It's a dichotomy of feelings now. It's an elite sorority. There's now a sense of pride about it all. But at the time, it was something I had to do. I was married and we needed to pay rent. It was scary doing it, I'll say that. I was eighteen. I was pregnant at the time I shot it, but I didn't know. It was shot by Lawrence Schiller, who was a *Life* sports photographer, and we shot it in his studio on Sunset Boulevard, an indoor shoot. There were a couple of things we did outdoors as well. If you look at the pictures, and look at the eyes, you will see absolute abject terror. I'll tell you one thing, posing for *Playboy* resulted in me being

chased around a lot more offices than I wanted to be. A lot of assumptions were made that shouldn't have been. There was one guy at 20th Century Fox who, for the purposes of litigation, shall remain nameless, who actually had a buzzer under his desk. When somebody went in for a reading, if he wanted to lock the door he hit that buzzer. It was actually a button.

Bikinis had just come in; it was really quite interesting, somewhat shocking. It was very hard on my career. It gave me notoriety that I could have done without, but did not help my career in films.

ABOVE: A rare photograph of a scene cut from the film in which Luther drags his sleeping bag back to the newspaper office. RIGHT: Attaboy Everett Greenbaum! BELOW: "Mr. Kelsey— YOU!" Luther discovers who has been behind the haunting.

film was made for under a million dollars. "Including studio costs, the whole thing cost about $700,000 and we made it fast. But do you know what really made that movie?" he asked in all seriousness. "The music."

To say the incomparable score by Vic Mizzy merely enhanced the film would be a massive understatement. The phenomenal orchestration includes one of the most memorable, infectious, unique—yet eerie—organ solos ever composed. It was the composer himself who had to sit at the mighty Wurlitzer and pump out the melody during the recording session.

"The organist we had in the session just froze. He wasn't used to working with pedals, too," Mizzy says.

Mizzy's music blasts out from the tip of the film, just as the swirling earth and Universal logo opens the darkened screen. It grabs you and sets a perfect tone for the comedy and flavor of the film. If ever there was a perfect marriage of action and music, this is it. The orchestration is something in between Mizzy's *The Addams Family Theme* and his score for *The Night Walker* with a dash of the same wild orchestra genius that Henry Mancini brought to his *Pink Panther* themes.

In his liner notes for the soundtrack CD of *The Ghost and Mr. Chicken* (Percepto Records), writer Daniel Schweiger beautifully captured Mizzy's contribution to the film: "Mizzy shows [his humor] right off the bat as the score erupts like a silent film overture over the Universal Pictures globe, its dark orchestrations promising something truly frightening. And just like that, Mizzy switches the theme into goofy percussion, accented with jazzy brass cries, xylophone runs, and the plucked strings of a fuzz guitar. . . . There are basically three themes that make up the bulk of *Mr. Chicken*'s score. But you wouldn't know it from the way that Mizzy blends and carries them to fit what's happening on-screen or in the characters' hearts."

Reviews

Variety: "*The Ghost and Mr. Chicken* is a silly, often funny, and entertaining mystery-comedy tailored to the talents of Don Knotts."

Los Angeles Times: "Besides being spooky and funny, it is also an appealing piece of Americana which has in Don Knotts a hero as delightfully feckless as Harry Langdon. . . . It remains as wistfully funny as ever in the talented hand of Knotts, whose high point is a painfully embarrassed speech

Charles Lane

Although he barely remembered working with Don Knotts in *The Ghost and Mr. Chicken* during a 1992 interview, character actor Charles Lane admitted that he couldn't remember half the work he'd done over the decades.

"It amazes me what people remember," he said when he was in his late eighties. "I can't remember anything. My memory is shot. It's just gone. I get residuals from things . . . I look at them and say, 'When the hell did I do that?'"

Fans may not have remembered his name, but they remembered his face. He'd been a recognizable character actor in films since the 1930s, and he became a memorable fixture on television after a few recurring episodes of *I Love Lucy* put him on the flickering screen. In the 1960s, he was a mainstay on TV's *Petticoat Junction* as the grumbling railroad executive, Homer Bedloe, eager to shut down Hooterville's depot. Beyond prolific, Lane amassed a list of film and TV credits that ran into the hundreds, parallel to few in his profession.

In *The Ghost and Mr. Chicken,* he was the perfect choice to play the hard-nosed lawyer, Mr. Whitlow. Recalls writer Everett Greenbaum: "Charlie was great in that role. Oh, Charlie, he smoked like a fiend. He had breath you could tap-dance on."

Lane was one of those traveling actors who popped up in films often, many times playing a similar type of humorous crank or stuffy landlord, businessman, or employer. He perfected the crusty skinflint.

"I was never under contract to a studio," he explained. "No, people in my bracket never were. The studios put people under contract with the potential of stardom. Young people, maybe they can build up into big moneymakers for them. But we, well they couldn't care less. So we ran around from one studio to another."

Charles Lane didn't stop smoking until he was nearly one hundred years old. He lived to the ripe old age of 102, and when he died, in 2007, he was the oldest card-carrying (founding) member of the Screen Actors Guild. He never won an Oscar or took home an Emmy for any of his illustrious career and, quite frankly, he said he didn't care.

before a picnic sponsored by the local chamber of commerce in his honor."

Hollywood Reporter: "Fine film humor, outrageous and wacky . . . a thoroughly delightful picture. It is solid gold farce, full of character and incident, that gallops along and quits a winner. Knotts is superb as the central character. His tortured face, his quivering frame, his spurts of false courage are all prime assets. . . . He is able to rein in these exaggerations to give reality and pathos to his affection for the leading lady. Joan Staley plays this role and gives it charm and beauty."

* * *

Let's Talk Chicken: Don Knotts Reminisces

Does The Ghost and Mr. Chicken *hold any passion with you?*

It sticks out because it was the first picture I did at Universal after leaving *The Andy Griffith Show.* I had a contract for five years and during the five years I made five pictures at Universal. I think it was one of the best.

There have been stories printed that you suffered a serious blood clot caused by filming scenes where you kept running up and down the staircase. Is this true?

That's a little wrong. I hurt my leg during the film; I think I pulled a muscle or something. But about a year later I got a blood clot; it wasn't related to that. It was a minor thing. But eventually, I had to watch it and not overdo it physically.

It's a wonder any of us lived through the movie. We had a tight schedule on that thing. We shot that in seventeen days. We were crazy to even try to do the movie in seventeen days, but we did. Of course we were working twelve-hour days, but even so, Alan Rafkin knew how to move a production along. Alan directed a lot of the *Andy Griffith* shows, which is why I got him over there. He's very fast and we knew we were gonna have to work fast.

Was Andy Griffith on the set with you?

Yes, as a matter of fact, the first wash treatment that we came up with for *Ghost* wasn't very good. We had a big meeting. A new producer came in, Ed Montagne. I asked Universal if they'd pay Andy Griffith to sit in 'cause Andy's a very good constructionist. We sat with Everett Greenbaum and Jim Fritzell and Andy and myself and sort of reblocked the story line. We spent about two weeks on that.

Mr. Chicken was released along with *Munster, Go Home!* as a double feature in theaters all around the country.

How did the line "Attaboy, Luther!" come about?

Everett [Greenbaum] had already written in "Attaboy, Luther" in that speech scene, and he's the one who yells it in the picture. It was Andy who said, "Why not have that guy as a running gag?"

After we screened the picture, somebody at Universal confronted us and said, "We think you should show the fellow who's been saying 'Attaboy, Luther' at the end of the movie." I said, "Are you kidding?" I really got mad. That was the dumbest suggestion I ever heard.

Weren't you responsible for the "and they used Bon Ami" line?

I don't recall that I wrote it, but there's a funny story about that. When we were writing and in the preproduction stage, I kept hearing from the legal department at Universal that the people at Bon Ami had not yet responded to their requests to use the product's name. I kept asking, "Have you heard from the people at Bon Ami?" and they'd shake their heads. It was such a good line I wanted to make sure it made it in the picture. Finally, I asked someone in legal if they minded if I called the people at the Bon Ami company and

THE INCREDIBLE MR. DON KNOTTS

LEFT: Celebrating the birthday of director Alan Rafkin on the set of *The Ghost and Mr. Chicken*. BELOW: Going over the next scene with director Rafkin.

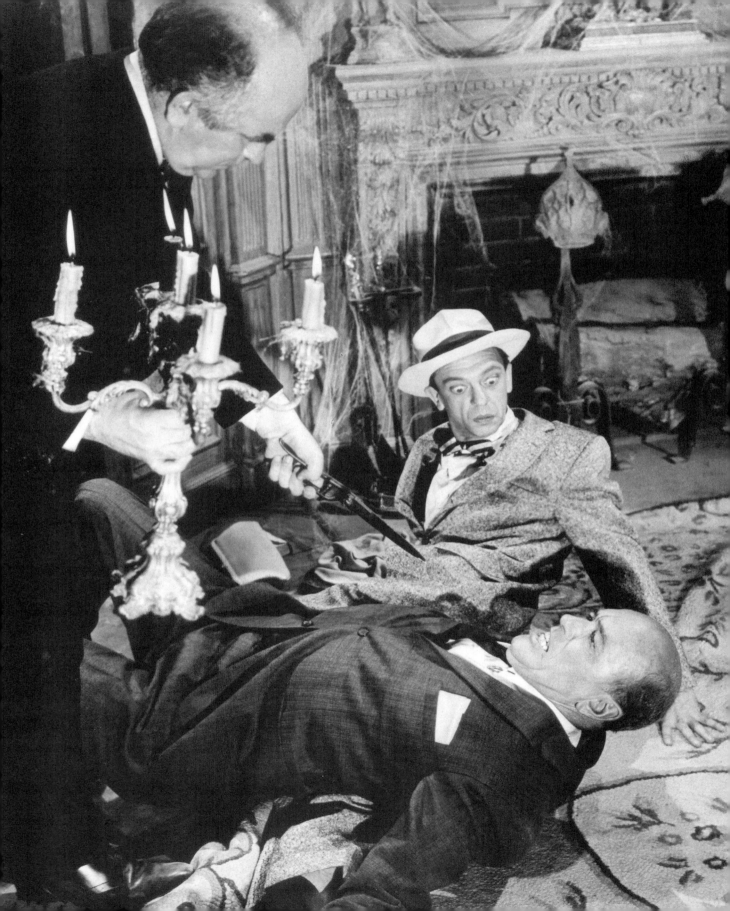

they said, "No, go ahead." I got on the phone and called the president of the Bon Ami company and explained what we wanted to do and he said, "Go right ahead . . . it sounds fun."

Were you proud of the way the picture came out?

Oh, yeah. I loved how it came out. I think the stuff in the haunted house was really fun to shoot and it looked great. And of course, Vic Mizzy's music is great. I've always enjoyed his work.

Tied Up and Knotts The secrets of the Simmons mansion are revealed.

Skip Homeier on Working with Don Knotts

As I recall it, Don was in an unusual place at that time in his life apparently. And I was expecting a guy who would be with the rest of the cast, which was an absolutely incredibly marvelous professional group of lovely people, all of whom got along perfectly. It was an extraordinarily pleasant situation, but from my point of view, Don was not part of that. He would come to work and he would work in the scenes and then he would lock himself up in his trailer and nobody ever saw him except under those circumstances. I can't really speak for the other performers, but we all went through the same situation. It was kind of unusual and it surprised the hell out of me because I thought he would be a different kind of cat. He just wasn't. He didn't seem to be having a very good time. He was extraordinarily intense. He just had something else going on in his life. His attitude or problems or whatever it was that kept him from kind of joining in, but it didn't affect anybody or make any difference. You just respected his position and did your work. He did his thing and we did ours. Everything about the show should have made it a great time. The material was enjoyable. The people all got along very helpfully with each other. We had a lot of laughs. A delightful professional cast, with his exception. He didn't socialize or say good morning or good night or let's go to lunch to anybody.

Sandra Gould

You may not remember the name, but there's no mistaking that *voice!* In *The Ghost and Mr. Chicken* she can be spotted as one of Mrs. Maxwell's fellow spiritualists, chanting, "Taro, Caro, Salamond!" But on television, Gould is perhaps best known for her nasal tone, abruptly shrieking "Aaaabner!" as nosy neighbor Gladys Kravitz on TV's long-running hit *Bewitched*. Sandra Gould's career spanned decades beginning in the early days of radio when she appeared on such programs as *My Friend Irma* and *Duffy's Tavern*. Those roles led to nearly fifteen years as a regular on Jack Benny's popular program.

On television Sandra appeared in *I Married Joan* and made two memorable guest appearances with fellow redhead Lucille Ball on *I Love Lucy*. While working onstage and doing voice-over work such as *The Flintstones*, her biggest break came in 1966 when she was asked to replace the late Alice Pearce in the role of Gladys Kravitz on *Bewitched*. (Actually, she was the producer's original choice for the role when the series premiered, but she couldn't accept due to family concerns.) She continued to play the hilariously intrusive snoop until the series ended in 1972. The character of Mrs. Kravitz was so popular that Sandra reprised her role in a short-lived *Bewitched* spin-off called *Tabitha.* Sandra worked by making guest appearances on television; one of her last roles was in a 1996 episode of *Friends* and one of her final appearances was on a segment of *Oprah!* She had been married to prolific television director Hollingsworth Morse.

Sandra Gould died on July 20, 1999, at age eighty-two. In the years shortly before her death, she had the opportunity to meet many of the fans whose lives were touched by her work while appearing at nostalgia shows with other *Bewitched* cast members. Something she was asked to do most often was to shout out her famous line ("Aaaabner! ") as loud as she possibly could. Heads turned, as she never refused.

—STEVEN COLBERT

Reta Shaw

Writers Everett Greenbaum and Jim Fritzell created the part of Mrs. Maxwell in *The Ghost and Mr. Chicken* with Reta Shaw in mind. She had been a favorite of theirs since 1953 when she first appeared as one of their characters, Aunt Lil, on the Wally Cox television series *Mister Peepers.*

Shaw happily claimed South Paris, Maine, as her hometown. She was born there on Friday, September 13, 1912. Shaw's earliest ambition was to become a missionary, but the stage beckoned. After training and stock experience, she decided to try her luck in New York at age twenty-six. When success eluded her, Shaw spent twenty-nine months overseas touring European army bases with the American Red Cross.

Shaw finally made her Broadway bow in 1946, subsequently appearing in three huge hits, *Gentlemen Prefer Blondes, Picnic,* and *The Pajama Game.* After filming the screen version of the latter, Shaw decided to make the West Coast her home. For the next eighteen years, she was very much sought after for the parts of domineering dowagers, authoritative nurses, and jolly housekeepers in both film and television. Television fans will recall her as Aunt Hagatha on *Bewitched* and as Hope Lange's trusted housekeeper in *The Ghost & Mrs. Muir,* and filmgoers will recall her portrayal of a melodious maid in Disney's motion picture masterpiece *Mary Poppins.* An imposing figure, the portly actress with cotton-white hair made her final film appearance in *Escape to Witch Mountain* in 1975.

Divorced from actor William Forester, Shaw made her home in North Hollywood with her daughter Kathy. She was active in her daughter's Girl Scout troop, assisted in PTA work, and enjoyed playing bridge. Reta Shaw died of emphysema on January 8, 1982, in Encino, California at the age of sixty-nine.

—FREDRICK TUCKER

Dizzying Notes: About Vic Mizzy

The incomparable Vic Mizzy began his association with Don Knotts in 1965 when he wrote the score for The Ghost and Mr. Chicken and continued a successful musical collaboration with The Reluctant Astronaut, The Shakiest Gun in the West, How to Frame a Figg, and The Love God? In his liner notes for the popular CD compilation Vic Mizzy Suites & Themes (Percepto Records), music critic Daniel Schweiger described the legendary composer's style with deserving verve:

Though he started out as one of the biggest, if popularly unrecognized songwriters of the 1940s, the stuff that Mizzy's best known for isn't playing on today's hep parade. His music has sunk into popular culture in a much deeper way, through the insidious instruments of film and television. Those who have heard the madcap harpsichord opening for *The Addams Family*, the funky organ concerto of *The Ghost and Mr. Chicken*, the rockin' surf music of *Don't Make Waves*, and the hayseed opening of *Green Acres* will never forget it. The music's so funky, so completely different than what stands for film and TV soundtracks, that you might just as well play it at cocktail hour.

Mizzy's music is a mad goulash of styles. In his world, fuzz guitars slam into harpsichords, sea shanties waltz with Mozart, and patriotic

Maestro extraordinaire Vic Mizzy, the genius behind the music in several Don Knotts movies.

bugles devolve into swinging jazz. A triple murder occurs onscreen, and the music treats it like Shirley Temple's strolling through Candyland. Someone talks about a clock and the music tick-tocks. For Mizzy, the musical hook is everything. The same theme keeps repeating with infinitely creative variations, most of which you can dance to. He's not so much scoring images as partying with them, the music just this side of a baroque Warner Brothers cartoon. Think Uncle Fester doing the Shag, and you'll hear Mizzy's unique, melodic sound, one better suited for a nightclub than the big or small screens. Many composers try to ape the vibe today with all the bells and whistles they can muster. Most don't come close.

"My music is very original and unpredictable," Mizzy says. "I never use conventional things. I'm what you'd call a 'spastic arranger.' You don't know how fast I compose these scores. The music hits me right then and there, and I'm usually right. If I deliberated how I wrote it, then the music wouldn't make it. I compose with a stream of consciousness.

"A lot of composers don't have a sense of humor, because they're writing wall-to-wall music," he comments. "The thing you learn

Vic Mizzy and studio musician Del Casher, who performed the "wah-wah" guitar sounds during the scoring session for *Ghost*.

about comedy is that you can't hit people in the ribs all of the time, like you would be if you were scoring a Bugs Bunny cartoon. The trick is to be very subtle with the scene. I would score the music before the joke, like having the music sound like a guy knocking on the door before he actually does it in the film. It's called 'preparing the cue.' That's one of my tricks, especially on comedies. I do these things because I have a wild and sordid sense of humor. You've got to have one if you want to score comedy."

Vic Mizzy today.

79

THE RELUCTANT ASTRONAUT

Released: 1967
Produced by: Edward J. Montagne
Written by: Jim Fritzell, Everett Greenbaum
Directed by: Alan Rafkin
Running Time: 102 minutes
Universal Studios

Cast

Don Knotts (Roy Fleming), Leslie Nielsen (Maj. Frank Gifford), Joan Freeman (Ellie Jackson), Jesse White (Donelli), Jeanette Nolan (Mrs. Fleming), Frank McGrath (Plank), Arthur O'Connell (Buck Fleming), Joan Shawlee (Blonde in Bar), Guy Raymond (Bert), Nydia Westman (Aunt Zana), Paul Hartman (Rush), Robert Simon (Cervantes), Robert Pickering (Moran), Pat Colby (Scientist), Marjorie Bennett (Woman at Mailbox), Jim Boles (Bartender), Paul Bradley (Man at Table), Paul Bryar (First Bus Driver), Ceil Cabot (Waitress), Al Checco (Console Operator), John Daheim (Startled Motorist), Fabian Dean (Second Bus Driver), Fay DeWitt (Secretary), Nick Dimitri (Astronaut), Jerry Dunphy (TV Newscaster), Cecil Elliot (Rosella Duncan, Woman with Dog), Pamelyn Ferdin (Mary, Little Girl in Spaceship), Med Flory (Tex, White Shirt in Bar), Vince Howard (Technician), Ray Kellogg (Brown Shirt in Bar), Dorothy Konrad (Aunt Harriet), Lee Krieger (Painter),

Astro-Knotts Roy's dad and friends make an unexpected visit at NASA.

Ralph Montgomery (Painter), Burt Mustin (Ned), Nelson Olmsted (Dr. Lowe), Bill Quinn (Capt. Ferguson), Don Ross (Airport Ticket Clerk), Billy Sands (Man Mopping Floor), Orville Sherman (Clerk), Herb Vigran (Dr. Bussart), Harry Holcomb (Dr. Bowan), Grant Woods (Technician), Thomas Bellin (Technician), William Hudson (Fireman), Loie Bridge (Frieda Wilcox), Robert Carraway (Earl Friendly), Mickey Finn (Charley), Murray Kamelhar (Technician), Jerry Dexler (Technician), Paul Grant (Technician), William Neff (Man), Eugene Pace (Man), Athena Lorde (Woman), James McHale (Photographer),

Knotts Landing Don proudly stands near the Apollo 1 Saturn rocket parked at its launch pad at Cape Kennedy in the summer of 1966. This rocket carried the crew of the first manned Apollo mission.

Don relaxes on the set of *Reluctant Astronaut* with Billy Sands, Everett Greenbaum, and Jim Fritzell.

Phil Montgomery, Budd Albright (Sailors), Clint Richie (Officer), Jimmy Stiles (Jordan), Jeff County, Cal Currens, (Ad Libs), Cindy Eilbacher, Christie Matchett, Linda Sue Risk, Debi Storm (Singing Girls)

Synopsis

In the small town of Sweetwater, Missouri, Roy Fleming works at the local fairground as the captain of a kiddie spaceship ride. Roy's proud father, Arbuckle Fleming, a former World War I corporal, submits an application to NASA for Roy to join the astronaut training program. One day, the news arrives that Roy has been accepted into NASA. Roy is petrified of heights (when he is finished with the kiddie space ride, he even requires help getting down from the rocket). He doesn't want to work at NASA. Unfortunately, his father never listens to him and does not give him the chance to explain himself.

Roy tries everything to get out of the job. Roy's girlfriend, Ellie, sees him off on his new vocation as well. He can't even bring himself to get on the plane ride there, so he ends up taking the bus. Eventually, Roy arrives at the manned space center in Houston and is placed in a janitorial program—not the astronaut training program. With his father and townsfolk so proud of him, Roy contin-

Ed Montague on Directing *The Reluctant Astronaut*

We had approval from Washington to shoot in Houston and then go to Cape Canaveral. When we got to Houston, we were turned off. Our contact, he was the voice of NASA, a PR guy who had worked for them and he was the publicity man. He said, "All you can do is shoot the exterior. . . ." I was rather shocked. We were going to be severely limited. Fortunately, our NASA contact from Washington was with us, and he made some calls and the word came. I was ready to leave and go to Cape Canaveral. I thought, *The hell with this. I'll go to Cape Canaveral.* Before we left, the word had come and we were able to shoot anything we wanted in Houston. We shot for a number of days in Houston and then went back to Cape Canaveral where they greeted us with open arms. As a matter of fact, they were getting ready the Apollo rocket, the one that eventually went to space, and that was the rocket that we shot in the picture.

There's a lot of me in [*Astronaut*]. Certain gags. I threw a lot of old Hal Roach gags in there, Don trying to feed himself, stuff like that.

In *Reluctant Astronaut*, I remember Don had hurt his leg and we were in the sequence where he's flying around in the capsule and of course, we had a harness made for him. I said,

"Don, you're going to do this, not the double." He said, "Okay, yes, no problem." Then when we were ready to do it, he decided he didn't want to do it. I had to go back and reshoot and put the helmet back on him so we could use a double with him flying around in the capsule who also had a helmet on to match.

ues the charade and lets everyone think he is training to be an astronaut.

One day, Roy sees his father, Buck Fleming, along with Plank and Rush on the closed-circuit TV monitor and realizes they are paying him a surprise visit at the NASA base. Roy quickly dons a space suit, pretends to be an astronaut in training, and gives them a grand tour. Bumbling Roy accidentally launches himself on a test rocket sled. Eventually, the mix-up is exposed to his father.

With Roy drowning his humiliation at a bar, a staff meeting at NASA declares the Russians are planning on sending a dentist to space to prove how safe their space program is. NASA counters they want to send a mission right away with the man least likely to fly to space. Roy's new friend, astronaut Gifford, recommends Roy for the mission. Roy is deployed to space in a rocket. When he accidentally gets peanut butter stuck in the guidance system, Roy's spacecraft is endangered and the mission may be aborted. Suddenly, Roy remembers the retro rockets from the amusement ride and launches them, remarkably sending the rocket home safely. Hailed as a hero, Roy decides to finally marry his girlfriend—but he just can't bring himself to get on that airplane for their honeymoon trip!

Behind the Scenes

The Reluctant Astronaut, the whimsical story of a timid man from the Midwest—afraid of heights, no less—winding up a trainee at NASA, premiered in Houston, Texas, on January 25, 1967. Ironically, just two days later, a tragic fiery accident occurred at Cape Kennedy on the launchpad when three astronauts (Virgil Grissom, Edward White, and Roger Chaffee) were killed during a preflight test for Apollo 1/Saturn 204, which was scheduled to be the first manned Apollo mission.

NASA's loss caused the country to mourn and much of the space program to be suspended pending investigations. The event caused Universal Studios to rethink their full-release campaign for *The Reluctant Astronaut.* After an ample amount of time, it was decided to proceed with the May release.

"There is no doubt in my mind but that the January tragedy at Cape Kennedy, where three Apollo astronauts died, has had an adverse effect on the business done by our second Don Knotts feature," said Henry Martin, vice president of Universal Pictures and general sales manager, in a story in *Variety. Astronaut* did not fare as well as Knotts's previous release, but Universal remained confident in the comedian's drawing power and ability to make movie audiences laugh, and they went forth with their next release, which was to take place in the Old West.

Sidelights

- Filming was completed on September 12, 1966.
- *The Reluctant Astronaut* held its world premiere in Houston, Texas, home of NASA, on January 25, 1967; the Los Angeles premiere was held on March 15, 1967. The film eventually hit 80 percent of the country in May 1967.
- Don Knotts's young son, Tom, appears as one of the kiddies in the space rocket at the opening of the movie.
- In March 1967, Don Knotts was cited by the United States Air Force and named "Honorary Recruiter." The title was bestowed on the comedian by Lt. Col. Robert R. Beaver, USAF recruiting chief for the Los Angeles area in a ceremony held at the Capitol Theatre in Glendale. Knotts was presented with a specially engraved model of the Thor missile.
- Associate producer Billy Sands has a bit part as a man mopping the floor.
- Baskin-Robbins Ice Cream Company created a special flavor for a promotion they called "Reluctant Astro-Nut."
- A coloring book based on the film (with brilliant artwork by prolific artist Bob Bentovoja on the cover) was released as a cross-promotion for the younger audience.
- Joan Freeman remembers: "Don was more of a quiet type. He really wasn't one of those comedians who was 'on' while on the set . . . just a very ordinary individual that you'd have a conversation with. Some comedians are entertainers and almost feel like they have to entertain. When I worked with the Three Stooges, they weren't trying to be funny, but sometimes they would do some very funny things inadvertently. That's because the three of them had worked together so much. He wasn't one who had to tell jokes like Danny Thomas. He was one of those types who needed to entertain the crew and the cast all the time."
- Leslie Nielsen remembers: "Don had just gotten married to a very attractive young lady and people kept on coming up to the booth where we were dining and bothering him to talk to him and he was eating. So I saw this attractive young lady who was married to him at that time, and she just put her hand out and rested it on Don's arm and pushed it down so he couldn't do anything with it and she said, 'We are very busy eating. Would you mind? We'll see you after dinner,' and Don was just laughing. We were having a good time. He was a very popular actor at the time, and a very funny actor. I wish I could have done more comedy then. Back then, producers saw me

The "Blast Off" Drinking Game

You Will Need

- ½   shot of amaretto almond liqueur
- ½   shot of 151 proof rum
- ¾   glass of beer of your choice (such as Bud Light, a standard blond beer or ale; not a dark beer)
- 1   DVD or videotape of *The Reluctant Astronaut*

Combine the amaretto and rum into a shot glass with the rum floating on top. Pour your glass of beer ¾ full. When ready, take the shot glass and drop it into the beer. Then, as the concoction begins to rumble like a rocket ship, guzzle down the entire drink. You'll love it—it tastes very similar to Dr. Pepper. (For a more impressive launch, you can ignite your fuel in the shot glass with a lighter or match before "blasting off" and dropping it into the beer. *Helpful Hint:* Make a pitcher or batch of the liquor concoction (½ amaretto and ½ rum) so you can readily pour the shots for the next scene.

Directions

Start the film and have a beer and your shot ready. The object of the game is efficiency: have your drink ready for each scene. Anytime during the film in which a character is seen holding a beverage, you must "blast off" and consume your drink in its entirety. And with each consumption, you must start a verbal countdown in honor of Roy. "5, 4, 3, 2, 1—ignition," drop shot into beer, then before guzzling the entire drink, you must also say, "Blast off!" as the drink begins to bubble. Most likely, by the end of this film you'll be in orbit.

Rule 1: If someone forgets to say any part of the countdown, ignition, and blast off, they are penalized with another drink that must be consumed.

Rule 2 (Optional): You must drop the shot with the right hand and drink with the left. If caught doing it wrong, another penalty of drinking.

Heads-Up Scene List

- Ellie holds a soda bottle in the hot-dog stand.
- Roy's dad and friends all have a beer.
- Roy gets a cup of coffee at the cafeteria.
- Drinks are consumed following the cutting of the cake.
- Buck Fleming holding a glass of some refreshment.
- The Blast Off Bar scene
- Mission Control employees are having some coffee.
- Finally one last toast at THE END.

Alternate Variation for Less Alcohol Consumption

Instead of using the beverage scenes as prompts to drink, try this: Every time Buck's friend "Rush" (Paul Hartmann) attempts to take a picture, consume your beverage. (This will happen only five times, midway through the film—and sometimes hurriedly.)

Have fun . . . but please, don't drink and drive.

as a straight leading man. I always wanted to do comedy. Nobody expected any comedy of me, so I played straight to Don's comedy."

- Vic Mizzy, while creating the film's score, composed a jaunty theme song for the opening. "I wrote a theme that went something like 'I don't want to go. I don't want to go. I don't want to go!'" Mizzy remembers. "I tried to have Don Knotts sing it, but that didn't work out." Instead, Mizzy went with a rollicking instrumental opening sans lyrics—a madcap theme so perfectly associated with the maestro and Don Knotts's films of the '60s.

Reviews

Variety: "Knotts, of course, has his comedy delivery and mugging down to a science and registers strongly. . . . A few comedy bits are run into the ground—the cow town airport loudspeaker, to name one—and Rexford Wimpy's Technicolor camera is often rooted in static setups. The climactic space flight, with a weightless Knotts floating about, is very amusing, but flawed slightly by holding too long, at least twice, on a shot which clearly shows the wires on his suit. . . . Overall, the pic will amuse the kids, but often will lose the attention of teenagers and older people."

The Hollywood Reporter: "[The writers] with Montagne doubling as director this time, have invested *The Reluctant Astronaut* with logical development that makes Knotts's incredible venture altogether plausible. Enhanced by unstinting production and rich characterization by a fine supporting cast, *Astronaut* will win its immediate rewards at the box office."

Leslie Nielsen (left) plays astronaut Frank Gifford, who attempts to sober up his plastered pal, Roy Fleming, in *The Reluctant Astronaut.*

THE SHAKIEST GUN IN THE WEST

Released: 1968
Produced by: Edward J. Montagne
Written by: Jim Fritzell, Everett Greenbaum, Frank Tashlin,
Edmund Hartmann
Directed by: Alan Rafkin
Running Time: 101 minutes
Universal Studios

Cast

Don Knotts (Dr. Jesse W. Heywood), Barbara Rhoades (Penelope "Bad Penny" Cushings), Jackie Coogan (Matthew Basch), Donald Barry (Rev. Zachary Gant), Ruth McDevitt (Olive), Frank McGrath (Mr. Remington), Terry Wilson (Welsh), Carl Ballantine (Abel Swanson), Pat Morita (Wong), Robert Yuro (Arnold the Kid), Herb Voland (Dr. Friedlander), Fay DeWitt (Violet), Dub Taylor (Pop McGovern), Hope Summers (Celia), Dick Wilson (Black Eagle Indian Chief), Vaughn Taylor (Rev. Longbaugh), Ed Peck (Sheriff), Edward Faulkner (Sam Huggins), Arthur Space (Sheriff Tolliver), Greg Mullavy (Phelps), E. J. Andre (Will Banks), Phil Arnold (Leonard, Photographer), Jim Boles (Big Springs Townsman), Argentina Brunetti (Squaw), Claudia Bryar (Mrs. Remington), Paul Bryar (Man at Bar), William Christopher (Hotel Manager), Frank Coghlan Jr. (Man at Bar), Jefferson County (Mr. Baker), Warde Donovan (Man), Mickey Finn (Father), Myron Healey (Stage Passenger Gambler), Charles Horvath (Drunk Indian Warrior), Anthony Jochim (Old Man), I. Stanford Jolley (Bearded Stage Passenger Army Scout), Sean Kennedy (Student), Gil Lamb (Drunk), Barbara Luddy (Screaming Woman), Kathryn Minner (96-Year-Old Woman), King Moody (Ernie), Burt Mustin (Old Artimus), Dorothy Neuman (Eva), Eddie Quillan

> " The West needs dentists. Teeth are falling out left and right out there. "
> —DON KNOTTS AS
> "DOC THE HEYWOOD"

(Porter), Bill Quinn (U.S. Marshal Bates), Teddy Quinn (Little Willie), Rodd Redwing (White Buffalo), Bruce Rhodewalt (Barber), Benny Rubin (Man at Bar), Leonard Stone (Bartender), Clay Tanner (Deputy), Jim Thayne (Bigson), Bruce Todd (Lyle), Helene Winston (Tillie), John Aniston (Indian), Jim Begg (1st Man), Ceil Cabot (Mother), Peggy Mondo (Indian Woman), Boyd Stockman (Stage Driver), Katey Barrett (Miss Stevenson), Tina Menard, Naomi Stevens (Squaws), Cal Currens (Scout), Matt Emery (Cowboy), Drew Harman (Student), Clyde Howdy (Man), Jimmy Joyce (Bystander), Ray Kellogg (Man), Athena Lorde (Old Mexican Lady), Stuart Nisbet (Older Man), J. J. Smith (Rider), Lorna Thayer (Bargirl), James McHale (Conductor #1), Phil Montgomery (Conductor #2), Vincent Barbi, Barry Brooks, Tom Dement (Cowpokes), Lee Krikorian, Joe LaCava, Irwin Mosley, Bob Harvey, John McKee (Cowboys), Jeff Malloy, Jason Heller (Students), Jimmy Stiles (Boy), Fred Catania, Jerry Okuneff (Backslappers)

ABOVE: Director Alan Rafkin sets up the shot with Barbara Rhoades and Don. BELOW: Jesse Haywood (Knotts) discovers dentistry is a real pain.

Synopsis

When timid Jesse W. Heywood graduates from a Pennsylvania dental college, he decides it's time to head out west to begin his frontier practice. As he makes his journey by stagecoach, the group he is riding with is robbed by two masked bandits, one of whom is pretty Penelope Cushings, alias "Bad Penny."

Penelope is captured by a sheriff's posse and agrees, in exchange for a full pardon, to aid the government in solving the mystery of who is smuggling guns to renegade Sioux Indians. In order to travel by wagon train, Penelope dupes Jesse into marrying her. (No single people are allowed on the wagon train.) The marriage is never consummated—but not because Jesse isn't willing. The Sioux attack the wagon train, much to Penelope's relief and poor Jesse's disappointment. During the attack, Jesse believes he is responsible for killing more than a dozen braves, when in fact it is Penelope doing the sharpshooting. Confident beyond belief, Jesse thinks himself to be the fastest

CLOCKWISE FROM TOP LEFT: Jesse swells with pride after repelling an Indian attack; a surprised winner in the showdown; the dentist must disguise himself as an Indian squaw to rescue his bride.

gunman in the West. When he finally confesses his lack of skills to the townspeople, he is immediately outcast. Jesse finally proves his worth when Penelope is captured by the Indians. By disguising himself as a squaw, he rescues his wife, helps her uncover the gun smugglers, and even gets in a few good shots all his own.

Sidelights

- Filming was completed on June 12, 1967.
- *Shakiest Gun* cost $1.2 million to produce.
- The film opened in Los Angeles on June 26, 1968.
- The title song was performed by "The Wilburn Brothers" who had a syndicated country-and-western television show in the 1960s.
- Writers Everett Greenbaum and Jim Fritzell thought it was perfect to throw the neurotic Knotts into a Western as a pioneer for modern dentistry. The

Jesse can't get married because he remembers that "Bad Penny" has not yet met his mother.

roots to this snaggletoothed feature film are long and winding. This film was a new twist on the old Bob Hope classic *The Paleface* (costarring Jane Russell) from 1948. Hope's movie, in turn, was a spoof of a 1946 film, *The Virginian,* with Joel McCrea and Brian Donlevy. This film was a remake of an early talkie Western of the same title, released in 1929 and starring Gary Cooper and Richard Arlen. All of this begot a 1960s television show called *The Virginian,* starring James Drury and Doug McClure, but let's not get into that.
- Knotts rounded up a posse of notable veteran character actors and comedians for this flick. Carl Ballantine (*McHale's Navy*) and Pat Morita (*Happy Days*) played proprietors of a general store who hornswoggle Knotts. Jackie Coogan (*The Addams Family*) portrayed one of the gunrunners, and Bill Christopher (*M*A*S*H*) played the hotel clerk.
- Also look for Dick Wilson, who for many years was "Mr. Whipple" ("Please don't squeeze the Charmin") on TV commercials, as the Indian chief. Wilson also portrayed the bandleader in *The Ghost and Mr. Chicken.*
- Actress Jennifer Aniston's father, John Aniston, portrays an Indian.

In Brief with Barbara Rhoades

Where was Shakiest Gun *in relation to your career?*

That was the second film I did. I came out from New York where I had done *Funny Girl* and I did a movie with Robert Wagner and Mary Tyler Moore called *Don't Just Stand There.* Then I was cast in *Shakiest Gun.* I didn't have a clue. It was a learning experience. I think I was nineteen. I was in awe of the whole situation. It was like going to school.

I didn't know how to ride a horse. They sent me to an equine center on the back lot where they had stables and took riding lessons, which didn't help a lot. At one point, I'm up in a wagon with a stunt driver and we're supposed to go racing out of town. We went to do the second take and Don came up to me and said, "Hey, you, get out of there! We need a double for you. Are you nuts?"

What do you remember about working with Don Knotts?

When I was cast, I had never met Don. He called me and picked me up and he took me out to dinner on Sunset Boulevard. I thought it was so Hollywood and fancy. He was the sweetest, nicest person. When we started to work, he made me laugh so hard. There were scenes where he would say something and the tears would roll down, I couldn't stop laughing. He'd look at me and I'd start laughing. People behind the camera were laughing away. He was so nice to me because he knew I didn't know from dirt what I was doing at the time and he looked after me and made sure I didn't get into trouble.

He was rather a frail person. He came in one day and he was sitting in the chair and I

look over and he's got these white stockings on up to his knees, like compression stockings. I asked him why he was wearing those and he said "I have very close veins."

Was the film a quick shoot?

We did it in twenty-three days in the back lot and we went out into the desert a little for the wagon-train scenes. All of the Indian camps

and such were on Stage 12. The very first thing we shot was the wedding-night scene. We're getting into the covered wagon. The going-to-bed scene, I remember. He goes somewhere to change and comes out immediately in his nightgown. They locked off the camera so they could do the quick cut. They had to match things and they had to teach me. It was a very fast learn.

- In one of the opening scenes, you'll notice the famous court-house and courtyard on the Universal Studios back lot, later famous as the setting in the *Back to the Future* films.
- Don Knotts uses his own real name in the beginning: Jesse.

Behind the Scenes

The film starts slowly with Knotts in an eastern dental school, attempting to coax a young lady to open her mouth. The gag drags on like a bad root canal. In a roustabout struggle with his patient, Don is obviously doubled by a stuntman who looks absolutely nothing like him. Momentum picks up when Don delivers a nerve-racked speech at the dental school's commencement exercises. After that, much of the film falls into a downward spiral of hokum and cheap gags—but perfect for the kiddies. It's not that the film doesn't have its moments. It does. Some of the funniest bits involve an eager Knotts as he learns he'll finally join his wife in bed for their honeymoon—only to be called away to night-watch duty for the wagon train.

Reviews

Los Angeles Times: "It's pleasant, ideal for kids who may not notice its chintzy look but just not up to par for Knotts. In the first two films [*Ghost* and *Shakiest Gun*] Jim Fritzell and Everett Greenbaum proved themselves to be among the best writers in town, but this time their muse deserted them out West amidst the cowboys and Indians."

Variety: "Universal has dipped into its remake barrel (via MCA ownership of the old Paramount pix library) to revamp the Edmund Hartmann–Frank Tashlin 'Paleface' script. A very wise decision, it serves Knotts to superior advantage, and works to introduce Miss Rhoades, a tall (5'11") titian-tressed newcomer with much acting ability already evident through her deft comedy performance."

THE LOVE GOD?

Released: 1969
Produced by: Edward J. Montagne
Written by: Nat Hiken
Directed by: Nat Hiken
Running Time: 101 minutes
Universal Studios

Cast

Don Knotts (Abner Audubon Peacock IV), Anne Francis (Lisa La-Monica), Edmond O'Brien (Osborn Tremain), James Gregory (Darrell Evans Hughes), Maureen Arthur (Eleanor Tremain), Maggie Peterson (Rose Ellen Wilkerson), Jesslyn Fax (Miss Love), Jacques Aubuchon (Carter Fenton), Marjorie Bennett (Miss Pickering), Jim Boles (Amos Peacock), Ruth McDevitt (Miss Keezy), Roy Stuart (Joe Merkel), Herbert Voland (Atty. Gen. Fredrick Snow), James Westerfield (Rev. Wilkerson), Bob Hastings (Shrader), Robert P. Lieb (Rayfield), Willis Bouchey (Judge Jeremiah Claypool), Herbie Faye (Lester Timkin), Johnny Seven (Petey), Joseph Perry (Big Joe), Jim Begg (Hotchkiss), Carla Borelli (Erica Lane), Nancy Bonniwell (Toma), Shelly Davis (Ingrid), Alesha Lee (Sherry), Terri Harper (Delilah), B. S. Pully (J. Charles Twilight), Pedro Gonzales Gonzales (Jose, Jungle Guide), Pitt Herbert (Minister), Carolyn Stellar (Madame).

Minor Parts and Bit Parts: Seamus Barrett, Vincent Barbi, Harry Brooks, Ethel Bryant, Lorelee Brown, Barbara Bosson, Ira Cook, Ian Carroll, Ceil Cabot, William Conklin, Frank Coghlan, Alan Craig, Frank Carroll, Barbara Dodd, Gina Dare, Lenore DeKoven, Marc Desmond, Glen Dixon, Jim Drum, Bill Dungan, Al Dunlap, Cecil Elliott, Frank Evans, Tony Franke, Rita Farnan, Fred Festinger, Dan Flynn, Lynn Fields, Jack Finch, Gerry Gaylor, Vic Hanson, Eddie Hanley, Bob Harvey, Patti Heider, Pitt Herbert, Chuck Horne, John Hubbard, Bo Johnson, Bernice Janssen, Urrea Jones, Jimmy Joyce, Elizabeth Kerr, Joe LaCava, Syl Lamont, Josephine Landis, Paula Lane, Lily Langley, Bonnie Lomann, Lori Lehman, Trent Lehman, Don Lucas, Larry McCormick, James McHale, James Macklin, Mike Mahoney, Shirley Melline, Frances Nealy, Cecile Ozorio, George Patton, Angelique Pettyjohn, David Reeves, Frieda Rentie, Vivian Rhodes, Araceli Rey, George Skinner, Billy Sands, Willi Say, Diane Sayer, Christopher Shea, Amber Marie Smale, Jeanine Sorel, Mike Steele, Bunny Summers, Carolyn Stellar, John Stuart, Yuki Tani, Eliza Ross Thorne, Elizabeth Talbot-Martin, Rita Quigley, Glen Vernon, Paula Victor, Vince Williams, Sunni Walton, Leslie York.

Ring-a-ding-ding! Peacock gets into the groove in *The Love God?*

Choir members: Betty Noyes, Doreen Tryden, Ada Beth Lee, Claire Gordon, Jean Detterman, Peggy Clark, Jo Ann Albert, William Days, William Reeve, Delos Jewkes, and Burt Dole. **The Blossoms:** Darlene Love, Jean King, and Fanita James. **The Orange Colored Sky Singers and Musicians:** Thurl Ravenscroft, Jack Virgil Skinner, Harold Lloyd Little, Neal A. Myers, Loren D. Cope, and Anthoney N. Greenstone.

Synopsis

Avian magazine publisher Abner Peacock's dream of capturing a photograph of the rarest bird in the world ("the South American Female Speckled Frecker, the *epicaris tropicaris*," in the jungles of Brazil) is nearly dashed as his beloved bird-watcher's magazine, *The Peacock,*

is in financial crisis and about to cease operation. Desperate to keep publishing, Abner Peacock hesitatingly takes on new partners: Osborn Tremain, his sexy wife, Eleanor Tremain, and a mobster by the name of "Ice Pick Charlie." With their own agenda in mind, the mobster and the Tremains need a fourth-class mailing license in order to publish their smut magazines, so they convince Abner to publish them. Newly hired editor Lisa LaMonica convinces Abner that the magazine will be classy.

Mr. Peacock becomes an unwilling sex symbol and celebrity.

Abner is taken to court on the charge of being a pornographer and he innocently becomes a hero for First Amendment rights. Somehow, he also becomes a national sex symbol and publisher—a Hugh Hefner–like figurehead. All of a sudden, Abner Peacock becomes a national craze and his Peacock Club opens in major cities across the nation: Chicago, Los Angeles, Miami, St. Louis, San Francisco. Peacock is the nation's swinger, with an entourage of lovely ladies who accompany him everywhere he goes. Still, Abner longs for the love of his old girlfriend back home, Rose Ellen (a preacher's daughter), and never forgets about his commitment to her. Rose Ellen has remained faithful, despite Abner's phenomenal rise to fame and power.

Despite herself, the magazine's editor, Lisa LaMonica, also grows fond of Abner. Mobster Ice Pick Charlie has his own ideas and gets in the way. Believing his own image, Abner decks the mobster and runs for his life.

Finally coming to his senses, Abner decides to shut the magazine down, but surprisingly his family is adamant about keeping the magazine going in order to make millions. All poor Abner wants is to get married to

Rose Ellen, settle down, publish his bird magazine, and resume his place within the church choir. You'll probably guess it'll be Lisa at the altar, but surprise, it's the devoted Rose Ellen who becomes Mrs. Peacock in the end.

Sidelights/Behind the Scenes

The Love God? was a vast departure from the homespun Americana G-rated flicks Knotts had been making at Universal. In this tangy sex satire, Knotts plays the publisher of a sensational *Playboy*-type magazine (more than one critic compared the main character with Hugh Hefner). Care was taken by Universal in their marketing of the film to clue in the public as to the different direction this film took compared to Knotts's usual fare.

Originally, Universal Studios was extremely enthusiastic about this Nat Hiken screenplay. Dick Van Dyke was an early choice to play Abner Peacock; however, Knotts eventually won out. Hiken, who had directed Phil Silvers in his popular *Sergeant Bilko* sitcom, desperately wanted the balding comedian to portray Osborn Tremain, the scheming smut publisher. After much coaxing, Silvers agreed to the role, but late in preproduction he bowed out for personal reasons. Silvers was replaced at the last minute by actor Edmond O'Brien—a choice that Hiken was not pleased with.

Bird magazine publisher Abner Peacock lets loose with a shrill birdcall in a South American jungle forcing his guide, José, to shudder.

- In the film's opening, the chorus is singing "Juanita," the song Barney Fife used to serenade his girlfriend in *The Andy Griffith Show.*
- In one press article, Knotts boasted that for this film he had a $15,000 wardrobe budget (extravagant for a male film lead at the time), including a leopard suit, a floral tapestry coat, and peacock pajamas.
- In addition to writing the screenplay, Nat Hiken (creator and director of *The Phil Silvers Show/Sergeant Bilko* and *Car 54 Where Are You?*) directed this film as well. He was a veteran comedy writer, having written for Lucille Ball, Milton Berle, and Martha Raye. Hiken was awarded an astounding eight Emmy Awards in his career, and *The Love God?* was his first motion picture. And, as it turned out, his last. Just days after principal photography for *The Love God?* wrapped, Hiken died suddenly at his home, the victim of a massive heart attack. He was just fifty-four.

Nat Hiken.

Gangster J. Charles Twilight (aka "Ice-Pick Charley") convinces Abner Peacock to think his way.

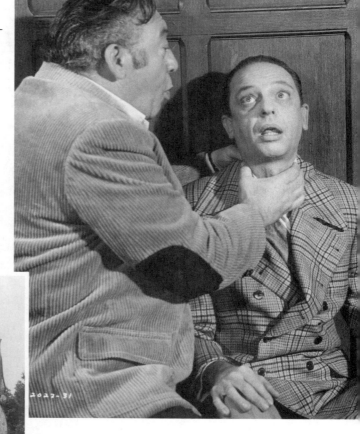

LEFT: Keezy (Ruth MacDevitt) lets Abner know she is disgusted by his new magazine. BELOW: Abner Peacock is tricked into becoming publisher of a risqué magazine in *The Love God?* OPPOSITE PAGE: Don tries on wardrobe.

- While the usual fantastic score by Vic Mizzy envelops the film, the score is augmented by two clever songs: "Mr. Peacock" (heard during the montage of Knotts's celebrity tour) and "Summer in the Meadow." "Mr. Peacock," written by Walter Slivinski and Nat Hiken, was performed by The Blossoms and featured strong vocals by singer Darlene Love. (Love, a former backup singer for Elvis, later scored a hit with "Christmas, Baby Please Come Home." The second addition to Mizzy's score was a cute number called "Summer in the Meadow," by Nat Hiken and Lyn Murray. This song was a salute to summer sung by a church choir, punctuated by Knotts's outrageous birdcalls. The chorus accompanying Knotts is Orange Colored Sky.

    One singer in the church chorus (unseen) is voice-over legend Thurl Ravenscroft, a basso profundo who provided the voice of Tony the Tiger in TV commercials hawking Kellogg's Frosted Flakes. Ravenscroft's other claim to fame was his rendition of "You're a Mean One, Mr. Grinch" in the animated *How the Grinch Stole Christmas!*
- The off-camera birdcalls were performed by voice-over actors Ginny Tyler and Dallas McKennon.

Sexy Maureen Arthur portrayed model Eleanor Tremain with great humor. Arthur married *Andy Griffith Show* producer Aaron Ruben.

Jesslyn Fax

Born January 4, 1893, in Toronto, Canada, Jesslyn Fax inherited a theatrical legacy. Her father, comedian and character actor Jimmy Fax, was the most famous entertainer in Canada at the peak of his career. Her uncle Reuben Fax was a noted Broadway actor at the turn of the twentieth century. At age sixteen, Jesslyn joined her father's troupe as a singer, pianist, and monologuist.

After five seasons with the group, Fax set out on her own for the United States where she performed in nightclubs, vaudeville, and traveling stock companies, none of which brought her fame or fortune. After her father's death in 1949, Fax made the leap to Hollywood, where soon her gnome-like face and quirky persona were in demand for film and television parts. She was a particular favorite of Alfred Hitchcock, appearing in both his films and television series.

Fax's most memorable films, besides *The Ghost and Mr. Chicken* and *The Love God?* include *Rear Window, The Music Man,* and *Paradise Alley.* Besides more than fifty guest appearances on television, Fax was a regular on three series, *Our Miss Brooks, The Ed Wynn Show,* and *Many Happy Returns.*

Never wed, Fax made her home in an apartment off Hollywood Boulevard. She spent her spare time sewing, studying metaphysics and hypnosis, and caring for five parakeets and a canary. She zipped around town in a little blue sports car, and her favorite place to shop for clothes was Frederick's of Hollywood.

Fax died in Woodland Hills, California, on February 16, 1975, following a stroke.

—FREDRICK TUCKER

Maggie Peterson on Filming *The Love God?*

Naturally, you had worked with Don Knotts on The Andy Griffith Show *as one of the Darlings. Had you done many films?*

No, *The Love God?* was the first movie I had been in with a substantial part. I was in a movie with Andy Griffith called *Angel in My Pocket,* but it was a small role. I think Andy suggested me for the role and I went over and talked to the director, Nat Hiken, and I got the part. I didn't have to read for it as such, but I had a little preliminary meeting.

It was a nice situation for me all the way through because I lived a block or two from Universal, so I could go home for lunch. And of course, I knew Don through the *Andy Griffith Show.* He and Andy were managed by my manager, Dick Link.

How did Nat Hiken and Don Knotts work together?

Nat and Don had a lot of laughs on the set and they seemed to enjoy each other's humor. In retrospect, Nat was fantastic, and a great humorist. He was a renowned comedy director and writer. Don is a little more subtle than that. I think the movie wasn't one of Don's best. When we were shooting it, it seemed a lot funnier. And fans didn't take to this movie like his previous movies. Not that I knew of beforehand. But afterward it became an issue. Maybe the timing of the movie. But afterward, it was an embarrassment to a lot of his fans I think, because they didn't see him in that light. Maybe it was a hair before it's time. There was an obvious parallel to Hugh Hefner. We knew it then.

What was Don Knotts like off the set?

Don's characters are so large, especially Barney, people often wonder about him personally. He was really shy, withdrawn I would say. He didn't match his characters in the life that I saw him. Never loud or boisterous.

He also enjoyed poor health. He was always sitting around with his legs up. I think he had phlebitis, or I thought he did. Something was always wrong. He was so tiny, a slight guy.

Here's something I remember that will give you an idea about what a kind man Don was. I was new and they had given me a guest-star billing. Not much more money, but I did get the billing, and that was part of my deal. And as such, I got my chair, a director's chair with my name on the back and it was on the set. This was a gentle and caring thing that Don did one day. There were a lot of extras on the set, and one day there was an extra sitting in my chair. And here I'm kind of shy and it was a new deal and I was excited to have my own chair. Don just sort of noticed me walking up to my chair and going around to the back of it, checking to make sure it was mine. And then he came over and told the guy that he was sitting in my chair. That was really a nice thing for him to do. I would have never asked the guy to get up. I would have gone and sat somewhere else. It shows his kindness.

Did you learn anything from the veteran character actors working in that film?

I remember Edmund O'Brien was at the end of his career at that time. He was a wonderful actor. They would bring him on and he would do his scenes and I would watch and I thought *Oh, my God . . . a train wreck.* I didn't know how they were going to make anything out of that. He was having trouble remembering his lines and having trouble seeing. I don't know if he was on medications at the time or what. That was my perception. However, when I saw the

Tying the Knotts Abner and his hometown girlfriend Rose Ellen Wilkerson (Maggie Peterson) finally get hitched at the conclusion of *The Love God?*

movie, he had film technique and he knew exactly what would be used on camera, so he saved up all his good stuff for the takes that he knew would be used. I thought he came off fantastic. Just goes to show that those old pros really knew their craft and knew what they were about. People like Spencer Tracy and Bette Davis. All of them knew what the camera did to them and what to use and what not to use. Don did, too. Andy Griffith was a master of that.

Mister Peacock is escorted around town by his sexy Pussy Cats: Sherry (Alesha Lee), Delilah (Terri Harper), Toma (Nancy Bonniwell), and Ingrid (Shelly Davis).

Reviews

The Hollywood Reporter: "In common with all of the Montagne-prouced Knotts comedies, *The Love God?* delights in outstanding casting of faces and characters down to the furthest background plane, reminiscent of the films of Frank Capra. Jesslyn Fax, a regular in this stock company, moves up to a featured billing in a delightful performance as a combination English tutor/FBI agent, and there are dependable bits of cantankery by the reliable Ruth McDevitt, James Westerfield, Jim Boles, and Jim Begg. James Gregory is just as fine as he can be—which is very fine—as the grandstanding defense counsel, Darryl Evan Hughes."

Variety: "*The Love God?* is the first of the Don Knotts-Universal—produced comedies to receive an M rather than a G rating from the MPAA. There are two scenes in which Knotts is pondering how, at a TV press conference, he's going to announce to the world that he's still a virgin. This is just one of several tasteless bits in a film which wastes the comedy talents of its star and featured players Anne Francis and Maureen Arthur."

Abner performs his signature birdcalls.

Ruth McDevitt

Like Reta Shaw, Ruth McDevitt was no stranger to working with Everett Greenbaum and Jim Fritzell, who wrote for the early 1950s sitcom *Mister Peepers*. On that show, McDevitt played the delightfully nerdy mother of the equally nerdy Wally Cox.

Born Ruth Thane Shoecraft in Coldwater, Michigan, on September 13, 1895, McDevitt had dreamed of becoming an actress as early as age seven. Although she graduated from the American Academy of Dramatic Arts while in her twenties, her physical appearance prevented her from nabbing any ingenue roles. She packed away her dream and got married. It was not until she was well past forty that McDevitt, using her late husband's surname, became a professional actress, making her Broadway debut in 1940.

Though only middle-aged, McDevitt was increasingly cast in grandmotherly roles, creating an image that stayed with her for thirty-five years. Besides an occasional television, radio, or film appearance, she was primarily a stage thespian until the final decade of her life, when she decided to move permanently to California. In fact, she made something of a career out of replacing her dear friend Josephine Hull in a succession of Broadway hits, including *Arsenic and Old Lace*, *Harvey*, and *The Solid Gold Cadillac*.

McDevitt's unsteady waddle and piping little voice were put to good use in nearly one hundred film and television appearances, including *The Parent Trap*, *The Birds*, and *Angel in My Pocket*. Her regular television roles included feisty Grandma Hanks in the ill-fated '60s TV sitcom *Pistols & Petticoats* and sweet Miss Emily in *Kolchak: The Night Stalker*. After a six-month battle with cancer, McDevitt died at her Hollywood home on May 27, 1976.

—Fredrick Tucker

HOW TO FRAME A FIGG

Released: 1971
Produced by: Edward J. Montagne
Written by: Don Knotts, Edward J. Montagne, George Tibbles
Directed by: Alan Rafkin
Running Time: 103 minutes
Universal Studios

Cast

Don Knotts (Hollis Alexander Figg), Joe Flynn (Kermit Sanderson), Edward Andrews (Mayor Robert Chisholm), Elaine Joyce (Ema Letha Kusic), Yvonne Craig (Glorianna Hastings), Frank Welker (Prentiss Gates), Bill Zuckert (Commissioner Henderson), Pitt Herbert (Dr. Schmidt), Robert P. Lieb (Commissioner Hayes), James Millhollin (Funeral Director), Fay DeWitt (Grace), Athena Lorde (Agnes), Bill Quinn (Asst. Atty. Gen. John Carmoni), John Archer (Gerard), Eddie Quillan (Old Man), Benny Rubin (Max), Billy Sands (Bowling Alley Manager), Clay Tanner (Motorcycle Officer), Al Checco (Bit)

Synopsis

Hollis Alexander Figg works at city hall as a trustworthy accountant. The mayor, Robert Chisholm, and many of his city officials are far from trustworthy, and they discuss ways to cover up their thievery from the city. Poor Figg is none the wiser. For protective purposes, they decide to fire all the bookkeepers, except one, and install a computer. They intend to retain Hollis (even promote him) as their patsy and put him in charge.

The next morning, Hollis is dumbfounded when he enters the office to find a massive computer next to his desk. He has been selected to operate the newly installed monstrosity. A few days later, Hollis is confused when he inserts figures into the computer and learns that a road built by the city had actually cost $500,000 when on the official books, it cost the taxpayers $750,000. When he accidentally stumbles upon the conflicting financial figures in the city's

TOP: Don Knotts and Andy Griffith pair on film in *No Time for Sergeants* (1958). ABOVE: Andy Griffith and Jim Nabors join Don on a network TV special.

THE FUNNIEST PICTURE SINCE FUN WAS BORN!

Mervyn Leroy
from the "NO TIME FOR SERGEANTS" and "MISTER ROBERTS"

Wake Me When It's Over

ERNIE KOVACS · MARGO MOORE · JACK WARDEN · NOBU McCARTHY · DICK SHAWN

SCREENPLAY BY RICHARD BREEN

CINEMASCOPE COLOR by DE LUXE

20. CENTURY-FOX

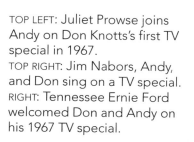

TOP LEFT: Juliet Prowse joins Andy on Don Knotts's first TV special in 1967.

TOP RIGHT: Jim Nabors, Andy, and Don sing on a TV special.

RIGHT: Tennessee Ernie Ford welcomed Don and Andy on his 1967 TV special.

RIGHT: A rare color photo of the lucky groom: Luther Heggs, from *The Ghost and Mr. Chicken.*
BELOW: "What is a guest speaker? . . . Let me clarify this."
BOTTOM: Perhaps the quintessential Don Knotts frozen scare take—the final moments from *The Ghost and Mr. Chicken.*

RIGHT: Actress Joan Staley today.
BELOW: Percepto records released several of Vic Mizzy's film scores on CD.

The Incredible Mr.Limpet

TECHNICOLOR PRE... DON KNOTTS · CAROLE COOK · ANDREW DUGGAN · JA...

The shakiest gun in the West with his weapon.

runaway hilarity when DON KNOTTS runs down CITY HALL...

the movie the entire family will enjoy!

HOW TO FRAME A FIGG

Featuring JOE FLYNN · ELAINE JOYCE · EDWARD ANDREWS · YVONNE CRAIG · FRANK WELKER
Screenplay by GEORGE TIBBLES Story by EDWARD J MONTAGNE and DON KNOTTS Directed by ALAN RAFKIN Produced by EDWARD J MONTAGNE · A UNIVERSAL PICTURE · TECHNICOLOR®

Scenes from *The Reluctant Astronaut*. ABOVE: Don and Joan Freeman in a quiet scene. BELOW: Inquisitive young Pamelyn Ferdin and Don.

The Apple Dumpling Gang.

Knotts and Conway became a bankable team in *The Apple Dumpling Gang Rides Again.*

In the seventies Don played with Gus and roamed Europe with Herbie.

Barney's back! In *Return to Mayberry.*

Don and Andy reunite for TV on *Matlock*.

Don holds an original Dave Woodman painting.

Don gets riled up in
Cannonball Run II.

An array of characters voiced by Don in animated movies: as himself in *The New Scooby-Doo Movies*, T. W. Turtle from *Cats Don't Dance*, Gee Willikers in *Pinocchio and the Emperor of the Night*, and Mutt Potter from *Tom Sawyer*.

Don received his star on Hollywood's Walk of Fame in 2000 and celebrated with family and friends including Andy Griffith, Betty Lynn, and Al Checco.

budget, he brings the paperwork straight to the mayor, who calls an emergency meeting of his cohorts. They work out a strategy to keep from getting caught—they will gain Hollis's trust by giving him a lavish office and a private secretary, while they ostensibly search out the crooks who have committed the crime.

Hollis Figg (Don Knotts) smashes his knuckles on league night in *How to Frame a Figg.*

Impressed, Hollis is immediately infatuated by his sexy private secretary, Glorianna, who lures him to her apartment and gets him inebriated. Stinking drunk, he ends up signing papers that he doesn't read. The secretary also manages to get him to break up with his girlfriend, who works at the local diner. At city hall, there is another panic meeting. It seems the attorney general's office is probing the situation. Glorianna frames Figg by testifying that Hollis has been giving her expensive furs and has put her up in a new apartment. When they open Hollis's own safe-deposit box, they conveniently discover $100,000 in cash. Hollis desperately tries to explain to his girlfriend that he's been framed.

Hollis extricates himself with the help of Ema and his trusted young friend Prentiss, a garbage collector. Together, they start an investigation. When one of the city officials drops dead, Hollis and Prentiss venture to the graveyard only to discover that the computer has been buried in a casket that is supposed to contain old Charley. By exposing the elaborate scheme, Hollis is finally cleared of charges.

Sidelights

- Filming was completed on April 17, 1970.
- LEO, the wall-sized computer, has a full name: Large-capacity Enumerative Officiator.
- Actor Frank Welker, who costars as Hollis's goofy friend Prentiss, eventually worked with Don Knotts again on the Scooby-Doo series for Hanna-Barbera Productions. Welker has been the voice of Fred since the animated series debuted in 1969.

Reviews

Variety: "The George Tibbles screenplay, based on a story by Montagne and Knotts, is a slick, yeoman job that leads by its own logic to Knotts and Frank Welker, his faithful friend the garbage

Joe Flynn

He once said, "I am a real jinx." And so it seemed as one of film's and TV's greatest second-bananas experienced several bruises in his career and life.

He was born on November 8, 1924, in Youngstown, Ohio. He attended Notre Dame for one year, then moved west and studied political science at USC. He entered show business and began pursuing stage roles, but he became disenchanted with the business and returned to the Midwest. After losing a bid to become a Republican state senator in Ohio, he headed out west and thought he'd give Hollywood a try again. After a rocky start (he was a ventriloquist and a radio deejay), his first feature film scenes in Alfred Hitchcock's *Rear Window* were thrown out. Later, he appeared in the films *The Seven Little Foys* and *Cry for Happy*, with television roles in between. Flynn first worked with Don Knotts in *The Last Time I Saw Archie* in 1961 and again in *How to Frame a Figg*.

Television was better suited for his unusual talents, as he found roles on *The Adventures of Ozzie and Harriet*, *The Life of Riley*, and *The George Gobel Show*. His comedy skills improved, and following some hilarious scene-stealing turns on *The Joey Bishop Show* in 1961, he was dropped. In 1962, his career sailed into high gear with his portrayal of hard-nosed spoilsport Capt. Wallace Binghampton on the ABC-TV sitcom *McHale's Navy*, opposite Ernest Borgnine. The painstaking art of comedy was just that for Flynn, and he frequently landed in the studio infirmary for cuts and bruises—even a broken rib.

Following his discharge from *McHale's Navy*, Flynn was seen floating the airwaves on such shows as *Batman*, *That Girl*, *Love American Style*, and *I Dream of Jeannie*. His career extended in diverse areas, as he played a nervous funeral director on Rod Serling's *Night Gallery*, hosted a game show called *It Pays to Be Ignorant* in 1973, and also provided the voice of King Vitamin in cereal commercials.

Disney Studios seemed to adore his comedic style and cast him in a series of popular films: *The Love Bug*, *The Computer Wore Tennis Shoes*, *Now You See Him Now You Don't*, *Superdad*, *The Million Dollar Duck*, and *The Barefoot Executive*. His final film for Disney was *The Strongest Man in the World*.

In his off-screen life, Flynn was a man who fought hard for the underdog, battling hard to secure residual payments for Screen Actors Guild members. While visiting South Carolina to deliver a speech for the American Cancer Society, Flynn was attacked, severely beaten, and robbed by two thugs.

The evening of July 18, 1974, he attended a wrap party for the completion of Disney's *Strongest Man* and the following morning, Joe Flynn's nude body was found floating in his Bel Air home's swimming pool. He had broken his leg weeks prior and was still wearing the cast. He decided to go wading in the early morning, suffered a heart attack, and drowned. He was only forty-nine years old.

The Strongest Man in the World was released five months after Flynn's death and one last Disney feature—an animated film called *The Rescuers*—marked the end of a twenty-year career in film and television.

—SAMMY KEITH

Edward Andrews

He was one of the most visible supporting actors on the small screen and the big screen in the '60s and '70s—mainly due to his effortless ability to play comedy and drama. Edward Andrews, the tall, bespectacled actor, was frequently cast as a banker, politician, corporate type, or senator.

He was born October 9, 1914, in Griffin, Georgia, to an Episcopal minister. He began his acting career on the stage when he was a teen, attended the University of Virginia, and eventually made it to Broadway in his early twenties. One of his earliest film roles was in *Elmer Gantry*, however, he is best remembered for his comedic roles in such films as *The Thrill of It All*, *The Glass Bottom Boat*, *Send Me No Flowers*, and *Sixteen Candles*. Andrews was no stranger to military roles, playing the defense secretary in both *The Absent-Minded Professor* and *Son of Flubber*. In the classic film *Tora! Tora! Tora!* he portrayed Adm. Harold C. Stark, and as a series regular, he played Comm. Roger Adrian on the short-lived sitcom *Broadside*.

His diversity in television is evident in the range of roles he played, from *Alfred Hitchcock Presents* and *The Twilight Zone* to *Bewitched*, *I Dream of Jeannie*, and *The Beverly Hillbillies*. Throw in a *Bonanza*, *Gunsmoke*, *The Untouchables*, and a *Quincy* and you've got quite a lengthy résumé. Some may recall his later portrayal as Jack Tripper's grandfather on *Three's Company*.

A husband and father of three, Andrews was an avid sailor and yachtsman who lived in Santa Monica, California, during his busiest years in Hollywood. He died on March 8, 1985, of a heart attack at the age of seventy. His final screen appearance was that of banker Mr. Corben in *Gremlins*.

—SAMMY KEITH

man, in a foggy graveyard at midnight digging up a computer named Leo programmed with the evidence to clear Knotts. Welker's character is a loyal and likable dumdum to whom life is a series of old movie clichés like, you know, Don Knotts in *How to Frame a Figg*."

Hollywood Reporter: "*How to Frame a Figg* will do very well at the box office. . . . Montagne has given it good physical production values on a modest budget and Rafkin has directed it tightly and quickly and without pretension so that the Knotts appeal is kept in the front. It is done without the obvious foolishness of some of today's comedians and even when in the most ludicrous situation such as digging a computer memory bank out of a grave retains a feeling of, if not probability, at least possibility."

ABOVE: Hollis, in drag as a grieving widow, tries to locate a buried computer in a casket as Prentiss (Frank Welker) fends off an old letch (Eddie Quillan). RIGHT: Flynn frames Figg.

THE INCREDIBLE MR. DON KNOTTS

Interview: Frank Welker

Was your costarring role in How to Frame a Figg *the first time you worked with Don Knotts?*

Actually, I was going over that in my head and I believe the feature was our first project together. We did some animation and a television show together. After the feature, Don asked me aboard as a cast member of his summer television show, *The Don Knotts Show*. So we worked together on several projects but never enough!

How were you cast opposite Don in the film?

Yes, I was cast as a costar, and since this was my first major role it was both very exciting and also a little scary. I was born in 1946, so that makes me sixty-two now, and I think I was twenty-two or twenty-three when we did *Figg*. I had appeared in a film for Stan Dragoti called *Dirty Little Billy,* and my credit was "Young Punk Buffalo Hunter number two"; needless to say it was not a very large role, in fact my credit was longer than my on-camera appearance! Also, I had worked with Elvis Presley in *Trouble with Girls* for MGM and I was working in a Disney feature with Kurt Russell when the reviews came out for *Figg*. I remember Michael McGreevy (one of our cast members) came into my trailer with the *LA Times* review and it was quite favorable to the film, Don, and myself. So I had worked on films but this was my biggest role.

You're so well known as a voice-over actor now. Were you aspiring to do more on-camera work back then? How did it affect your career?

I started out wanting to be a star, then a dramatic actor, then an actor, then I realized that my on-camera acting was not coinciding with my ambition. I did do quite a bit of on-camera; besides the films, there were commercials and pilots. I did one pilot with Richard Dreyfuss where I had a very nice role as the pilot who kept crashing airplanes, Captain Pace in Joseph Heller's *Catch-22*. That year they also had a competing pilot, *M*A*S*H*. I still wonder how my career would have been different had the network picked us. They didn't, and the reason, I understand, was it was too expensive to do as a weekly series. Anyway, though *Figg* was a great experience it didn't really do anything to help my on-camera acting ambitions. I gave up my desire for dramatic acting when I did a death scene for a CBS casting director and a room full of producers and writers. I remember being in the middle of the room on the floor wrenching pain and agony from my imaginary bullet wound. All of that emotion and inner turmoil brought resounding laughter from the all the powers and pencils on the sofas. It was then I dedicated myself to my first love . . . comedy!

Did you and Don work well together? Your character was a bit "dumber" than his . . . was it intimidating to act next to this comedy great?

Well, the way we were playing it, Prentiss Gates was more socially unaware and was zooming through life at full capacity . . . slim, dumb and happy. But the two guys really liked each other, and Prentiss would pick up on the obvious that the much more educated but obtuse Hollis Figg just didn't see. Yes, it was a little like dumb and dumber.

I was a bit nervous working with Don at first. He was not very open or outgoing . . . let's just say he was shy and reserved. He was always very polite, and I think when he found out that I was inexperienced he went out of his way to be friendly and helpful. He would make sugges-

Elaine Joyce, Don, and Frank Welker crack up during the filming of *Figg*.

tions on ways to play the scene or how I could help set him up better than what the director suggested. We became good working friends and I always was and remain in awe of his great gifts as a comedy actor. I also had deep respect for him as a person.

Did you have a favorite scene working with Don in the film?

I think the graveyard scene. Don and I came up with a bit where he cupped his hands to assist me in getting over the wall I was about to climb. He bends down, cups his hands and I blindly jump up on the wall and climb over . . . Don is left standing there with his hand cupped bent over and I am gone. The look on his face says it all.

There is something that I call a "library laugh." It occurs when you start to giggle at something and then you cannot control your laughter, and it snowballs. There was a scene at the breakfast table with Don, Elaine Joyce, and yours truly. It was a simple scene. We were discussing some information we had gathered for some plot exposition. I don't know how it began, but we started giggling, and by the time we blew four or five takes we were completely out of control . . . the director couldn't

even say, "roll 'em" and we were in spasm. Poor Ed Montagne, after about ten ruined takes he was forced to yell at us, "Act like professionals and get serious; we have a comedy to do!"

When Don guest-starred twice on Scooby-Doo, *did he join the cast for the recording sessions?*

You know I was trying to put all of that together in my mind and figure out the timeline. I think we worked one of those sessions together, but if so, it would probably have been before *Figg* I think. . . . I can't remember; aren't you glad I'm not keeping the top secret telephone number for the president's red phone!!!!?

114

THE MAN WHO CAME TO DINNER

Original Broadcast Date: November 29, 1972
Produced by: Duane Bogie, Sam Denoff, Bill Persky
Written by: Moss Hart, George S. Kaufman, Sam Denoff, Bill Persky
Directed by: Buzz Kulik
Running Time: 90 minutes
NBC-TV: Hallmark Hall of Fame presentation

Cast

Orson Welles (Sheridan Whiteside), Lee Remick (Maggie Cutler), Joan Collins (Lorraine Sheldon), Don Knotts (Dr. Bradley), Edward Andrews (Ernest W. Stanley), Marty Feldman (Banjo), Peter Haskell (Bert Jefferson), Mary Wickes (Nurse Preen), Elisabeth Welch, Michael Gough

Synopsis/Sidelights

This is an updated version of the immensely popular 1939 George S. Kaufman/Moss Hart comedy that played to rave reviews on Broadway. Orson Welles plays blowhard Sheridan Whiteside, the legendary acid-tongued lecturer/author/critic, who comes

Don and the great Orson Welles on the set in England during the production of the *Hallmark Hall of Fame* special "The Man Who Came to Dinner."

to dinner in a small Ohio town and is injured when he slips on his host's doorstep. Forced to convalesce at the home in a wheelchair, he wreaks havoc on the entire household and seemingly takes over the neighborhood. This television adaptation, produced by Universal Television with Foote, Cone & Belding Productions and NBC-TV, is a production of the *Hallmark Hall of Fame* drama series—the oldest and most honored drama series at the time, having earned more than forty Emmy Awards when this program aired.

Behind the Scenes

- According to Orson Welles, he had been offered the role of Sheridan Whiteside in both the original stage production and the 1942 film; he later said he was "very smart [to have declined]; because if you've seen the film you'll know it was awful and there was no way for anybody to be good in it."
- Prolific character actress Mary Wickes got her big break on Broadway playing the overwhelmed Nurse Preen, a funny role she played for more than two years during the show's original

Mary Wickes.

run and on tour. She and Monty Woolley were the only stars of the Broadway production to be cast in the 1941 Warner Brothers motion-picture adaptation, which costarred Bette Davis, Jimmy Durante, and Billie Burke. Thirty years later (and a multitude of nurse, housekeeper, and Catholic nun roles later), Wickes recreated her harassed "Nurse Preen" role for this TV movie.

- Although this TV version of the famed play takes place in Ohio, the entire production was videotaped in Southampton, England, in late 1972 for broadcast in America on NBC Television. According to Don Knotts: "Orson Welles, who lived in Paris at the time, was apparently having some tax difficulties . . . and didn't want to return to the United States to do the show, so it was videotaped in England." The show's cast rehearsed for three weeks in London and taped over a period of three days in Southampton.

- In his 1999 autobiography, *Barney Fife and Other Characters I Have Known* (cowritten with Robert Metz), Don Knotts explains that this was one of his most memorable and cherished experiences in the business—to be working next to Orson Welles. The two became inseparable during the monthlong process, mostly talking about their common interests in magic, Harry Houdini, and old movies. Knotts found Welles to be intriguing as well as fragile. Welles drank wine heavily during the rehearsals and had difficulty remembering his voluminous lines, thus requiring cue cards during certain scenes. The production was plagued with a flu bug, which hit several cast members. That, coupled with the temperament of Welles, who constantly bickered with director Buzz Kulik, caused things to get tense. Welles, who by that time was quite obese, demanded the air conditioner be cranked up so the studio felt like an icebox; some cast members were off to the side of the stage bundled up in blankets and overcoats waiting to make their entrances. Knotts recalled:

> My scenes were with Welles, and he called me aside and whispered directions to me. His suggestions were, of course, brilliant. Welles was a genius. There is not much question about that, and I felt honored to be the recipient of his personal direction. . . .
>
> On the first day of taping, Mr. Welles arrived bright and early, sober as a judge, and full of vim and vigor. He was a whole new person.

Just as he was about to tape my biggest scene, Buzz came out of the control room to have a word with Welles. They got into a terrible fight, and they began screaming at each other. Buzz stormed into the control room and Welles looked at me plaintively. Shaking his head, he said "Don, we have no director." Then Buzz's voice came over the loudspeaker. "All right," he yelled, "let's tape this!" *Oh boy,* I thought to myself, *what a way to go into my biggest scene.* Thankfully, it seemed to go off without a hitch. . . .

Except for the long hours and the fact that the British crew almost refused to stay overtime on the last night to finish the show, the entire taping went off pretty much without incident. I flew home tired and happy.

Reviews

Variety: "Joan Collins was marvelous as the sexpot movie star, Edward Andrews was excellent as the unwilling host, Mary Wickes's re-creation of the nurse role was a pleasure, Michael Gough contributed an elegant cameo as a bitchy Britisher, Kim Braden stole her scenes as a dotty old lady, and Don Knotts was perfect in playing his established mealy mouthed character. None of the others in the extensive cast was less than good."

Animated
Episodes: "Guess Who's Knott Coming to Dinner?" and
"The Spooky Fog"
Produced by: William Hanna, Joseph Barbera
Directed by: William Hanna, Joseph Barbera
Running Time: 43 minutes
Hanna-Barbera Productions
Aired: CBS-TV

Cast

Don Knotts (Himself), Don Messick
(Scooby-Doo), Casey Kasem
(Norville "Shaggy" Rogers),
Frank Welker (Fred
"Freddy" Jones),
Heather North (Daphne
Blake), Nicole Jaffe
(Velma), Michael Bell,
Joe Besser, Daws Butler,
Henry Corden, Larry
Harmon, Pat Harrington
Jr., Ted Knight, Jim Mac-
George, Alan Oppen-
heimer, Mike Road,
Olan Soulé, John
Stephenson, Vincent
Van Patten, Lennie
Weinrib, Sherry
Alberoni, Jillian Ann
Durgin, Joan Gerber,
Florence Halop, Cindy Put-
nam, Janet Waldo

Synopsis/Sidelights

*   While driving along in the famous
    Mystery Machine van, Scooby Doo
    and the gang (Fred, Daphne, Shaggy,
    and Velma) happen upon Don
    Knotts and attempt to
    unravel a mystery that
    surrounds them.

Scooby and Shaggy continue their unending quest for food, all the while dodging ghosts and creatures around nearly every corner and through frequent mine shafts.

- *Scooby-Doo, Where Are You?* was introduced to Saturday morning audiences in the fall of 1969 and became an immediate hit. Patterned after characters from the popular CBS sitcom *The Many Loves of Dobie Gillis* (adding a talking Great Dane), *Scooby* became a cultural institution and megahit for Hanna-Barbera's animation team. In its third season, the format was altered to fit an hour time slot and the title became *The New Scooby-Doo Movies.* This new program featured a string of surprise special guest stars, including Don Knotts, Phyllis Diller, the Three Stooges, Davy Jones, the Harlem Globetrotters, Jonathan Winters, Tim Conway, Laurel and Hardy, Sandy Duncan, Sonny and Cher, Jerry Reed, Cass Elliot, Dick Van Dyke, Don Adams, Batman and Robin, Speedy Buggy, Josie and the Pussycats, and the Addams Family. The series lasted two seasons and produced twenty-four episodes.

- The episode "Guess Who's Knott Coming to Dinner" aired October 7, 1972. The gang discovers Don Knotts at Moody Manor. Knotts disguises himself in wacky outfits—including in drag—in an attempt to trick the gang. The search is on for the elusive Captain Moody.

DON KNOTTS

61-2

"GUESS WHO'S KNOTT COMING TO DINNER"

© Hanna-Barbera Prods. 8/1/72

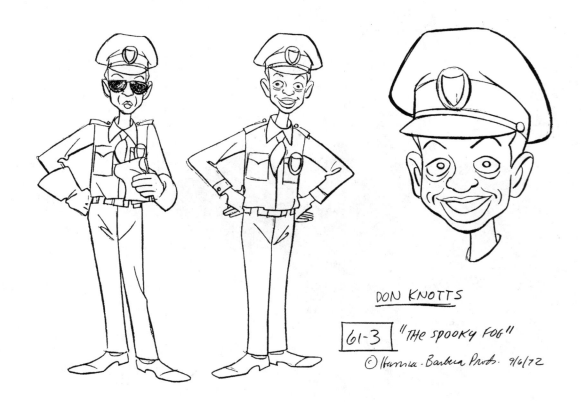

DON KNOTTS

61-3   "THE SPOOKY FOG"

© Hanna-Barbera Prods. 9/6/72

Animators perfectly captured the essence of Don's face for his appearances on *Scooby-Doo*.

DON KNOTTS DISGUISED AS
SHERLOCK HOLMES
61-2 "GUESS WHO'S KNOTT COMING TO DINNER"
© Hanna-Barbera Prods. 8/1/72

DON KNOTTS DISGUISED AS
SMORGASBORD THE SWEDISH MAID
61-2 "GUESS WHO'S KNOTT COMING
TO DINNER"
© Hanna-Barbera Prods. 7/31/72

- The episode "The Spooky Fog" aired November 4, 1972. The gang discovers Don Knotts working as the deputy in the friendly ghost town of Juneberry. Knotts introduces them to sheriff Dandy Taylor, and the references to *The Andy Griffith Show* continue from there.
- Frank Welker, the voice of Fred, costarred with Knotts a year earlier in *How to Frame a Figg*.

I LOVE A MYSTERY

Released: 1973
Produced by: Frank Price
Written by: Carlton E. Morse, Leslie Stevens
Directed by: Leslie Stevens
Running Time: 120 minutes
Universal Studios

Cast

Ida Lupino (Randolph Cheyene), Les Crane (Jack Packard), David Hartman (Doc Long), Hagan Beggs (Reggie York), Jack Weston (Job Cheyne), Don Knotts (Alexander Archer), Terry-Thomas (Gordon Elliot), Melodie Johnson (Charity), Karen Jensen (Faith), Deanna Lund (Hope), Andre Philippe (Andre), Francine York (Telegram Girl), Peter Mamakos, Lewis Charles

Ida Lupino, Jack Weston, and Don Knotts costarred in *I Love a Mystery.*

Synopsis/Sidelights

- Jack, Doc, and Reggie are insurance investigators and adventure seekers who travel to a remote island mansion to solve a mystery. A billionaire is missing, and his wife may or may not be telling the truth. The plaintive wails of a mysterious baby, kidnapping, and even murder contribute to the mystery. The missing man's lovely daughters, Faith, Hope, and Charity, sometimes get in the way of the investigation for the three intrepid heroes. The script for *I Love a Mystery* was based on an old radio serial called *The Thing That Cries in the Night.* As it happened, this movie (actually a pilot for a TV show) sat on the shelf for seven years before it finally aired. Although Don Knotts is advertised as one of the film's stars, he merely shows up to sputter one forgettable line at the end of the film.
- *I Love a Mystery* was produced as a movie/TV pilot for Universal Studios.

THE APPLE DUMPLING GANG

Released: 1975
Produced by:
Written by: Jack M. Bickham, Don Tait
Directed by: Norman Tokar
Running Time: 100 minutes
Walt Disney Productions

Cast

Tim Conway (Amos Tucker), Don Knotts (Theodore Ogelvie), Harry Morgan (Sheriff Homer McCoy), John McGiver (Leonard Sharpe), Bill Bixby (Russell Donovan), Don Knight (John Wintle), Susan Clark (Magnolia "Dusty" Clydesdale), David Wayne (Col. T. R. Clydesdale), Stacy Manning (Celia Bradley), Clay O'Brien (Bobby Bradley), Brad Savage (Clovis Bradley), Slim Pickens (Frank Stillwell), Dennis Fimple (Rudy Hooks), Pepe Callahan (Clemons), Iris Adrian (Poker Polly), Fran Ryan (Mrs. Stockley), Bing Russell (Herm Dally), James Brodhead (The Mouthpiece), Jim Boles (Easy Archie), Olan Soule (Rube Clarke), Tom Waters (Rowdy Joe Dover), Dawn Little Sky (Big Foot), Joshua Shelley (Broadway Phil), Richard Lee-Sung (Oh So), Arthur Wong (No So), Dick Winslow (Slippery Sid), Bill Dunbar (Fast Eddie), Wally K. Berns (Cheating Charley), Bruce Kimmel (Bank Teller), Larry Vincent (Townsman)

Synopsis

In the summer of 1879, a handsome gambler named Russell Donovan rides into the town of Quake City, California, en route to New Orleans and a healthy poker game. When he loses his last dollar, he is cornered into taking care of a family of orphaned kids: twelve-year-old Bobby, seven-year-old Clovia, and Celia, age five. Desperate, he tries to palm off the kids and shirk his responsibility. The kids prove to be trouble right from the start and initially don't take to Donovan. The little ones call themselves the Apple Dumpling Gang.

Into town roll a pair of bungling desperadoes, Theodore Ogelvie and Amos Tucker, who call themselves the Hash Knife Outfit. They make a play on the bank, but their hapless attempt at robbery fails. When the kids discover an abandoned gold mine and a massive gold nugget, suddenly everyone in the town wants to be their guardian. The judge orders that only a married couple may adopt the orphans. Hastily, Donovan marries a lady stagecoach driver named Dusty, intent on getting his hands on the treasure. The kids, sensing the situation, run away and hide out; while hiding, they meet the Hash

Knife duo. The kids convince Theodore and Amos to rob the bank and steal the gold so Donovan won't want the loot. So, Theodore and Amos throw in with the young Apple Dumpling Gang and proceed to rob the bank . . . again.

When the newly expanded Apple Dumpling Gang arrive at the bank for their heist, they discover it's already being robbed by another band of outlaws. Suddenly, everyone is scrambling to steal the prized giant gold nugget. A shoot-out ensues and rumbles the whole town. The gold, well, it gets blown to bits in an explosion and everyone is eagerly picking up the tiny pieces scattered throughout the little town. In the end, Donovan and Dusty become the proud parents of the young Apple Dumpling Gang. As for Theodore and Amos, the reformed Hash Knife duo head out for a better life in the countryside.

The Bradley kids (Clay O'Brien, Stacy Manning, and Brad Savage) join forces with the Hash Knife Outfit (Knotts and Conway) to locate gold in mine.

Behind the Scenes/Sidelights

- This film marks the debut teaming effort of Don Knotts and Tim Conway. Knotts, ten years older than Conway, had to reinvent his performance on film. Playing a pair of bungling bank robbers, both comedians had styles all their own. At least they thought so.

  "We walked down the street for our first shot," said Conway during the production. "The director Norman Tokar stopped us and said, 'You boys are doing the same kind of comedy walk. One of you has to change it.' Don and I know each other's work so well that all I had to say was, 'You use the number six walk with the three face, and I'll do the number four walk with the two face.'"

  Eventually, their characterizations were cemented and the two comedians began a long film association with this Disney starter. Knotts decidedly wished to set free the character of the "nervous little guy" and branch out with something new. "I got the feeling of being boxed in, stuck with the same character," he told a reporter during the production. His character is a much bolder, riskier type than in previous films. Taking on the numskull role this time was Tim Conway, who played it stupid most

A Visit with Tim Conway

Had you seen Don Knotts perform before you two worked together?

I was a big fan of the old *Tonight Show* with Steve Allen and as a matter of fact, Don was probably one of the reasons I'm in this business. I thought that if I wanted to do anything in this business, I wanted to have the attitude that Don had. Of course, those were much more innocent days. He enjoyed entertaining. He was kind, he was Mayberryish. He was this silly gentle little guy, a friendly guy. His comedy was friendly and his audience loved him for that. He was a charmer. I often thought I'd like to have that same opinion of the business and comedy that Don did.

Do you think your styles were compatible or did you have to make major adjustments when working with Don Knotts?

Our styles were compatible because we both thought alike. When we did things together, I don't think either one of us was the straight man. We were both comics who appreciated each other's attack or approach to comedy. One of the important things in comedy is knowing when to shut up, and we both knew when to shut up. There's a couple of things in the movies that went wrong. Neither one of us broke up, so it just kept playing. The ladder business in *The Apple Dumpling Gang.* We never really worked that whole thing out until they actually had set up to shoot it. Don and I just kind of walked around with this stupid ladder and he knew enough that when I pulled on the ladder to stop or to go or whatever. All of that business of crawling over the guy and running into bells was just kind of adlibbed. He knew exactly what to do to make it funny and never to stop and question, "Hey, what are we doing here?" He had a great funny bone.

Don could just look at me and make me laugh. He had the same effect on me that I had on Harvey Korman. You could read his face. That little smile that told you that he understood that you understood that I understood that you understood . . . you know? I loved being around him and he enjoyed laughing.

Were you attempting to create a movie comedy team?

We enjoyed working with each other, but we weren't going after a team. After I started doing Vegas and different theaters around the country with Harvey Korman, a lot of times Harvey wouldn't be able to make a trip or he would be ill, and Don would step in, so we worked a lot in clubs, too. Don was one of those reliable guys. We never really targeted becoming a team. It would be like Laurel and Laurel, you know?

I wrote *The Prize Fighter* in a day and a half and *The Private Eyes* took a little longer. I wrote them intending that Don and I would work together. Writing for Don was so easy.

Don didn't like performing stunts, did he?

I'm pretty athletic and was a boxer in high school and college. I never put Don in any danger. He was kind of a chicken that way. He always saw the danger in scenes and avoided it. He'd had a blood clot in his leg at one time, which is obviously very dangerous, and he assumed that if he had one, there must be others. And he didn't put himself in any kind of jeopardy, and that's why with anything that he could be injured, he had a stunt double. He didn't want to end his life by jumping off a wall.

Did you have a favorite film with Don?

I think my favorite was either *The Prize Fighter* or *The Private Eyes* because a lot of things were a surprise to him. For instance, when I threw the pigeon through the window in *The Private Eyes,* Don didn't know I was going to do that. And if you'll notice when you look at it, he just stares at this thing. He didn't break up. He just stares at it like you would in real life and then gave me that stupid look. He could encourage laughter by just looking at you.

Why did you two stop making films together?

There was no conscious decision to part ways. Had I come up with another, I'm sure we would've been able to work it out. We had a lot of success with those movies, and I guess we should have done more. I'm not sure why we didn't. Later on, Don and I voiced some characters together on the *Hermie* cartoon series that came out on videotape.

Once Don had the problem with his eyes, it became very difficult for him to work. He really couldn't stand being under lights. That really bothered him. Even in natural daylight, it bothered him.

When did you last see Don?

Several months before he passed away. I would call him and leave messages. He got to the point where he didn't really answer the phone much anymore. He didn't want to discuss what was going on and I think, outside of Andy and Tom Poston, I don't think he really had much to do with people toward the end. He just got away from it. I called a lot and left a lot of messages. I used to call just to call his answering machine because his voice was on his service.

of the time. The chemistry between the two jelled well between them and audiences, paving the way for future teamings.

"At first," admitted Knotts to the Associated Press in 1974, "we thought we were too similar . . . and couldn't work together. But we found out that wasn't true because each of us has something different to bring to the character we're playing. It's really fun to work together in another comedy with a guy who's really funny. Like, if I'm not so funny in a particular scene, he will be. It's similar to Laurel and Hardy in some ways."

Amos and Theodore plot the possibility of a sequel.

- For an authentic touch, much of the Technicolor location shots were captured in the Los Padres and Deschutes National forests in Oregon.

- Midget actor and stuntman Jerry Maren was clad in a little girl's white dress and rode the buckboard as it went sailing out of control. Maren, doubling for the youngest actress, said he "nearly got killed" as the contraption gained speed and came to a halt, throwing him. His wife, Elizabeth Barrington, also a little person, was standing in and performing stunts for the youngest boy and can be seen in the runaway mine car. (*Trivia:* Jerry Maren began his career in Hollywood as the Lollipop Munchkin in *The Wizard of Oz*.)

- Don Knotts recalled a few behind-the-scenes moments filming *Apple Dumpling Gang*: "Just walking around in a cowboy suit was kinda fun," he added. He remembered working with the young kids. "Well, little kids aren't too seasoned at that age. I remember she [Stacy Manning] had trouble squinting at the light; every time she had a scene, she'd start and [the director] would say, 'Don't squint, honey, don't squint.'"

- Knotts was terrified of anything involving a stunt. "If there is anything falling or blowing up, Don is not there," says Tim Conway. Knotts explained: "I have never done a stunt in my life, you might say, which gets to be kinda funny because if I had to jump off the top step, if it's two steps down, I got a stunt double in there."

- "Of all the pictures I made for Disney," Knotts admitted, "*The Apple Dumpling Gang* was the most fun I ever had. It was just terrific."

- One of the reasons the children in the cast shine so much in this film is certainly because of the talents of director Norman Tokar, who was experienced at working with young actors. A veteran of ten previous Disney film hits, Tokar also spent several years directing episodes of TV's *Leave It to Beaver* at Universal Studios.

Clay O'Brien, thirteen, was the oldest of the trio portraying sibling orphans in *The Apple Dumpling Gang.* O'Brien probably came to the film with the most acting experience. His father (Gene O'Brien) was a film stuntman. He began working in Westerns, his first film being *The Cowboys* starring John Wayne. Freckle-faced Brad Savage, eight, worked in more than fifty commercials before landing the Disney film. Stacy Manning, six, the blue-eyed blonde cutie in the cast, had just a few commercials to her credit before being cast in the film.

Two of the former child actors remember working on *The Apple Dumpling Gang* on the film's DVD extras. Brad Savage recalls, "Don Knotts was actually quite shy and a gentleman and very nice and friendly, but you would expect him to be kooky and crazy off-camera but he wasn't at all." Clay O'Brien adds, "My favorite scenes to work in were the ones with Tim Conway and Don Knotts. You had to kinda watch what you were doing or you would get caught up in what they were doing and then you'd bust up laughing and ruin the scene and they'd have to do it over again."

Reviews

Los Angeles Herald-Examiner: "Disney films traditionally promote an unshakeable faith in the mystical power of a child's grin (or, better yet, his tears) to recharge the good-buy batteries of adults who've grown up and too far away from childhood. *The Apple Dumpling Gang* is no exception."

Cinnamon Apple Dumplings

If you've never heard of, or even tried apple dumplings, then you're in for a treat with this sumptuous dessert. Make a batch for the family and pop in the movie to add to the flavor. Now that's an evening. You'll love 'em.

2	TABLESPOONS BUTTER, MELTED
1¾	CUPS SIFTED ALL-PURPOSE FLOUR, DIVIDED (SIFT BEFORE MEASURING)
2	CUPS APPLE JUICE
¾	CUP GRANULATED SUGAR, DIVIDED
1½	TABLESPOONS CINNAMON CANDIES (SUCH AS RED HOTS)
3	MEDIUM APPLES, CORED AND SLICED BUT NOT PEELED
2	TEASPOONS BAKING POWDER
¼	TEASPOON SALT
½	TEASPOON GROUND NUTMEG
2	TABLESPOONS VEGETABLE SHORTENING
⅔	CUP WHOLE MILK
	ABOUT 1 CUP HEAVY CREAM, FOR SERVING

Stir together melted butter and ¼ cup flour in a 10-inch skillet or shallow pan that has a tight lid. Gradually stir in juice, blending until smooth. Stir in ½ cup sugar. Cook over medium-high heat until thickened, stirring constantly. Add cinnamon candies and apple slices; bring liquid to a boil, then reduce to a simmer.

Sift together remaining 1½ cups of flour, baking powder, salt, remaining ¼ cup sugar and nutmeg. With a pastry blender or two knives, cut in shortening until mixture resembles coarse meal. Add milk; mix only until all flour is dampened. Dip a tablespoon into cold water, then use the spoon to drop dough into the hot syrup. Repeat with the remaining dough, dipping spoon into water as necessary. Simmer uncovered for 10 minutes, then cover tightly and simmer 10 minutes more or until dumplings are cooked through. To serve warm dumplings, place apples and syrup into bowls; pass cream at the table.

YIELD: 8 SERVINGS

Boxoffice: "Three young children and a large cast of veteran talent go through their paces in tried and true Disney fashion, this time in a comedy-western vein. . . . Families who enjoy Disney movies should have no complaints here."

Variety: "*The Apple Dumpling Gang* turns the cinema pages back to those happier family-entertainment days when a film was directed at this former type of mass divertissement and could live by its own merits. Endowed with the sort of ingredients that preceded the need for MPAA ratings, latest Disney release is an engaging gentle-humored comedy melodrama of three orphans set down in an early California community . . . should rack up satisfactory returns."

"Following The Apple Dumpling Gang, I made five more features for Disney over the next four years. . . . Nobody gets rich working for Disney, but I had a lot of fun."
—DON KNOTTS

NO DEPOSIT, NO RETURN

Released: 1976
Produced by: Ron Miller, Joe McEveety
Written by: Joseph L. McEveety, Arthur Alsberg, Don Nelson
Directed by: Norman Tokar
Running Time: 112 minutes
Walt Disney Productions

Cast

David Niven (J. W. Osborne), Darren McGavin (Duke Mayfield), Don Knotts (Bert Delaney), Herschel Bernardi (Sgt. Max Turner), Barbara Feldon (Carolyn Osborne), Kim Richards (Tracy Osborne), Brad Savage (Jay Osborne), John Williams (Jameson the Butler), Charles Martin Smith (Det. Longnecker), Vic Tayback (Big Joe Adamo), Bob Hastings (Peter the Chauffer), Louis Guss (Freddie), Richard O'Brien (Capt. Boland), Barney Phillips (Sgt. Benson), Ruth Manning (Miss Murdock), Olive Dunbar (Mrs. Hadley), James Hong (Ming Lo), Jean Gillespie (Sandy, a Reporter), Jack Wells (Reporter), Stu Gilliam (Policeman at Airport), Jack Griffin (Officer Henderson), Milt Kogan (Policeman), Hank Jones (Banana Cop), Iris Adrian (Housewife), Henry Slate (Cement Truck Driver)

Synopsis

During Easter vacation from school, young Tracy Osborne, age eleven, and her brother, Jay, age nine, don't know where to turn. Their widowed mother, Carolyn Osborne, is in Hong Kong on a business trip once again, and they are being shuffled off to California to visit their wealthy grandfather, J. W. Osborne. Their grandfather is not interested in the young ones and isn't looking forward to their visit—and the kids feel the same way. After a debacle at the airport caused by Jay's pet skunk, the grandfather sees his grandchildren make off in a taxicab occupied by two rusty safe-crackers, Duke Mayfield and Bert Delaney.

The kids talk their way into staying with Duke and Bert, who are trying to pull one last caper in order to pay off a debt they owe to gangster Big Joe Adamo. Their grandfather allows the kids their adventure to teach them a lesson and relieve him of his duties. He has secretly stationed a watchman opposite Duke's apartment for their protection.

Tracy launches a plan to raise money for Duke and Bert as well as airfare for her and Jay to fly to Hong Kong to surprise their mother. She mails a ransom note to her grandfather stating that she and her brother have been kidnapped and can be returned for $100,000. Tipped off by his watchman, the grandfather is amused by the ploy and responds with a letter of regret in lieu of the ransom.

When Big Joe comes to collect his money, the kids have sprung traps on the gangster to avoid capture. Big Joe finds out about the kids and ruse and wants in on the kidnapping caper. Eventually the police get involved with the whole situation. The chief investigator has been on the trail of famous safecracker Duke for years and is determined to solve the case and get the children back. When the kids become locked in their grandfather's walk-in safe, Duke saves their lives by using his talents to open the airtight vault in the final hour.

Darren McGavin and Don Knotts make a fairly decent comedy team in this funny Walt Disney caper, *No Deposit, No Return*.

Sidelights

- The original title for this film was *Double Trouble*.
- The Los Angeles premiere for this film was held on February 11, 1976.
- *No Deposit, No Return* successfully pairs Don Knotts and Darren McGavin as a couple of bungling safecrackers who take up kidnapping to make some easy cash—but it turns out to be not so easily accomplished. The teaming of Knotts and McGavin, as unconventional as it sounds, actually played well on film—a bit like Abbott and Costello in style. Knotts performs more physical gags in this film than ever before. "I spent a lot of time dangling

LEFT: Safe cracker Bert Delaney (Don Knotts) chases after a skunk. BELOW: Clever kids Tracy and Jay Osborne (Kim Richards, Brad Savage) finagle the inept safe crackers (Knotts and McGavin) into a kidnapping scheme.

THE INCREDIBLE MR. DON KNOTTS

from girders, falling off buildings, and getting pushed out of cars," he said at the time. "I like to do visual comedy, but I don't take chances. When it comes to really dangerous stuff, I let the stuntmen take over and then I walk in for the close-up. . . . You go home stiff and sore and bruised up a little bit, but if the laughs are there it's worth it."

- Young Brad Savage, nine at the time, previously worked closely with Knotts in *The Apple Dumpling Gang* as Clovis Bradley, the kid who disliked being touched.

Reviews

Los Angeles Herald-Examiner: "There's nothing much in *No Deposit, No Return* we haven't seen lots of times before. . . . A particularly talented, hardworking crew of actors keeps things from going soggy."

Los Angeles Times: "McGavin, in an unaccustomed kind of casting, manages the difficult jobs of being a reluctant criminal, funny but not clownish, and sympathetic enough to be a possible love interest for Miss Feldon. . . . *No Deposit, No Return* is the kind of well-engineered and undemanding comedy the studio by now can turn out in its sleep."

Evening Outlook: "Knotts delivers his standard portrait: the timorous good-hearted sidekick. Knotts has an unusual ability to get great mileage out of trivial schticks. Witness his shot-nerves routine with a cup of coffee and spoon. . . . Unfortunately, Knotts is thrown into several extended slapstick sequences, the longest of which not only is poorly done, but also completely irrelevant to the plot."

"Oyach!"

Released: 1976
Produced by: Ron Miller
Written by: Ted Key, Arthur Alsberg, Don Nelson
Directed by: Vincent McEveety
Running Time: 96 minutes
Walt Disney Productions

Cast

Edward Asner (Hank Cooper), Don Knotts (Coach Ernie Venner), Gary Grimes (Andy Petrovic), Tim Conway (Crankcase), Louise "Liberty" Williams (Debbie Kovac), Dick Van Patten (Cal Wilson), Ronnie Schell (Joe Barnsdale), Bob Crane (Pepper), Johnny Unitas (Himself), Dick Butkus (Rob Cargil), Harold Gould (Charles Gwynn), Tom Bosley (Spinner), Titos Vandis (Papa Petrovic), Hanna Hertelendy (Mama Petrovic), Liam Dunn (Dr. Morgan), Virginia O'Brien (Reporter), Kenneth Tobey (Asst. Warden), Irwin Charone (Hotel Clerk), Timothy Brown (Calvin Barnes), Jackson Bostwick (Stjepan Petrovic), John Orchard (Pemberton Captain), Richard Kiel (Tall Man), Henry Slate (Fan), Larry McCormick (N.Y. Broadcaster), Larry Burrell (Locker Room Announcer), Danny Wells (Referee), James Almanzar (Coach Garcia), Milton Frome (Lukom), Iris Adrian (Fan's Wife), Bryan O'Byrne (Grocery Store Manager), Jack Manning (Mayor), James Brown (Mammoth Coach), Warde Donovan (Butcher), Jeanne Bates (Nurse), Dick Enberg (Atoms' Announcer), George Putnam (TV Interviewer), Stu Nahan (L.A. Sportscaster), Fred Dryer (Atoms Player—Sidelines & Shower), Bowman Upchurch (Binocular Man in Press Box)

Synopsis

Hank Cooper, owner of the hapless California Atoms football team, is headed for another losing season. The aging cheerleaders fail to draw attention. Even head coach Ernie Venner can't quite help the situation.

Meanwhile, on a farm in the Yugoslavian countryside, Andrija "Andy" Petrovic is upset because he can't compete with his soccer-

star brother Stjepan. Andy's mule, named Gus, shows his sports prowess by kicking the soccer ball with great intensity. It soars out of sight! Andy sees the chance to finally win his papa's respect . . . by way of the mule.

Thinking such an act might pep up the crowds at least, Cooper flies Andy and the mule to the United States to be part of the halftime show. On a whim, Cooper throws the mule into the game as an official player. The rules are checked and since they never specify that the word "player" is restricted to humans, Gus is in the game. Gus helps the team win repeatedly and they are on their way to the Super Bowl. A pair of inept thieves are hired to kidnap Gus and hide him until after the big game. When an impostor mule adorned with fake markings is brought in, of course, nothing happens and it's inevitable that everyone will look like a jackass. With just minutes left in the game, the real Gus is found and must be transported to the game by helicopter and lowered onto the field for the final play. Gus misses the ball, but Andy grabs it and runs 106 yards for a touchdown—winning the Super Bowl!

Sidelights

- The Los Angeles premiere was held on July 7, 1976.
- The film is based on an idea by famous cartoonist Ted Key, who also created the cartoon strip *Hazel*, which inspired the television series starring Shirley Booth in the 1960s.
- Watch for appearances by football personalities Johnny Unitas, Dick Butkus, and announcer Dick Enberg.
- Gus the mule was twelve years old, which is equivalent to sixty human years. Gus was thirteen hands high and weighed seven hundred pounds. His trainer was Bobby Davenport with assistance by Donald Crow. Gus worked in additional films, but this was his first starring role.
- Trivia: The movie shown at the drive-in was *Million Dollar Duck* (1971), also directed by Vincent McEveety.
- This was actor Bob Crane's final motion picture appearance. The actor was murdered in 1978.
- Actor Jackson Bostwick, who portrays the star soccer player back in Yugoslavia, played the superhero *Shazzam* on the live-action Saturday morning TV show in the 1970s.

" *Gus* was one of my first films because at that time I was strictly steeped in television. Don was such a pleasure. He had the same bug-eyed look as an agent I had in New York. He had so much comic talent and he had some of the funniest moments, all ground down to Don. He had me peeing in my pants. "

—ED ASNER

Reviews

Variety: "Only Walt Disney Prods would dream of doing a film about a mule that kicks field goals for a pro football team. . . . *Gus* is a pleasant family comedy which both kids and parents will enjoy. . . . *Gus* has the amiable spirit of a tall tale or kiddie story book, and while the plot mechanics are largely predictable, the cast keeps the ball in the air over the 96-minute running time."

Los Angeles Times: "*Gus* is a funny and loveable, though familiar Disney live-action fantasy film for football families about a mule from Yugoslavia who salvages a sagging L.A. gridiron by kicking 100-yard field goals. . . . On the whole, *Gus* is zippy, lighthearted and engaging entertainment for all those who wish to believe in magical mules."

MULE FEATHERS

Released: 1977
Produced by: Robert F. Slatzer
Written by: Donald R. von Mizener
Directed by: Donald R. von Mizener
Running Time: 90 minutes
Harry Weed Productions/BAM Productions

Cast

Don Knotts (Voice of Mule), Rory Calhoun, Richard Webb, Angela Richardson, Doodles Weaver, Noble "Kid" Chissell, Nicholas Worth, Arthur Roberts, Cathy Carribu, Theodore Lehman, Dee Cooper, Nedra Volz, Dorinda Carey, Patrick Crenshaw, Ken Smedberg, Frank Otterman, Ruth Vinson, Ken Johnson

Synopsis/Sidelights

- *Mule Feathers* is an obscure independent film produced by BAM Productions. Rory Calhoun, in one of his final film roles, stars as an outlaw masquerading as a parson in this Old West satire. The film was originally titled *The West Is Still Wild* and was filmed in June 1975 on the Paramount Ranch in Southern California as well as locations in Arizona.

- This is one of the least seen Don Knotts films for sure. Narrated by Knotts, this film concerns an itinerant preacher who travels the countryside in the company of a hilarious talking mule (also the voice of Don Knotts) and eventually joins a search for hidden gold treasure that turns into a close encounter with an angry, grizzled Rory Calhoun. This independent PG-rated movie was completed in 1977, but unfortunately it was put on hold and was eventually aired on a pay-cable movie channel, which is probably the reason it isn't that well known. It was released as *Mule Feathers* on VHS in the 1980s.

This mule will kick you off your Blazing Saddle!

Scheduled For Release July, 1978

MULE FEATHERS

STARRING **RORY CALHOUN**   VOICE OF NELSON THE MULE BY **DON KNOTTS**

Angela Richardson • Richard Webb • Dee Cooper • Cathy Carricaburu •
Doodles Weaver • Noble "Kid" Chissell • Frank Otterman

Written and Directed By Donald R. Von Mizener   Animated By John Paul Jones
Produced By Robert F. Slatzer   Associate Producer Ross Hawkins

Harry Weed Productions
822 North La Cienega Boulevard, Los Angeles, California 90069 • (213) 652-5254

HERBIE GOES TO MONTE CARLO

Released: 1977
Produced by: Ron Miller
Written by: Gordon Buford, Arthur Alsberg, Don Nelson
Directed by: Vincent McEveety
Running Time: 105 minutes
Walt Disney Productions

Cast

Dean Jones (Jim Douglas), Don Knotts (Wheely Applegate), Julie Sommars (Diane Darcy), Jacques Marin (Inspector Bouchet), Roy Kinnear (Quincey), Bernard Fox (Max), Eric Braeden (Bruno Von Stickle), Xavier Saint-Macary (Detective Fontenoy), Francios Lalande (Monsieur Ribeaux), Alan Caillou (Emile—Chief Inspector), Laurie Main (Duval—Diamond Guard), Mike Kulcsar (Claude), Johnny Haymer (Race Official), Stanley Brock (Taxi Driver), Gerard Jugnot (Waiter), Jean-Marie Proslier, Tom McCorrey (Showroom MC), Lloyd Nelson (Mechanic), Jean-Jacques Moreau (Truck Driver), Yveline Briere (Girlfriend), Sebastien Floche (French Tourist), Madeleine Damien (Old Woman), Alain Janey (Man at Cafe), Raoul Delfosse (Police Captain), Ed Marcus (Exhibit MC), Dick Warlock (Driver), Jerry Brutsche (Driver), Carey Loftin (Driver), Bob Harris (Driver), Jesse Wayne (Driver), Bill Erickson (Driver), Regis Parton (Driver), Kevin Johnston (Driver), Josiane Balasko, Andre Penvern (French Policeman), and, of course . . . Herbie the Love Bug

Synopsis

Race-car driver Jim Douglas and wily mechanic Wheely Applegate arrive in Paris with Herbie, their zippy 1963 Volkswagen Beetle, for the first annual road race from Paris through the French Alps to Monte Carlo. Unbeknownst to them, two museum thieves named Max and Quincey make off with a magnificent diamond and clumsily hide the gem in Herbie's gas tank. Renowned police inspector Bouchet is on the case. In reality, his alter ego is "Double X," the mastermind behind the jewel theft.

The brand new Love Bug turns the great race into a HERBIE-DERBY!

WALT DISNEY PRODUCTIONS' **HERBIE** GOES TO MONTE CARLO

Starring Dean JONES, Don KNOTTS, Julie SOMMARS Co-Starring ROY KINNEAR, JACQUES MARIN, XAVIER SAINT MACARY, FRANÇOIS LALANDE Written by ARTHUR ALSBERG and DON NELSON Based on characters created by GORDON BUFORD Music by FRANK DE VOL Produced by RON MILLER Directed by VINCENT McEVEETY TECHNICOLOR® [G] GENERAL AUDIENCES Released by BUENA VISTA DISTRIBUTION CO., INC. ©1977 Walt Disney Productions

When in California, enjoy new Space Mountain at DISNEYLAND. When in Florida, visit The Vacation Kingdom WALT DISNEY WORLD

Herbie falls head over wheels in love with a cool baby-blue Lancia Scorpion sports car driven by lovely Diane Darcy, who wants nothing to do with Jim and Wheely. She intends to win the race. Meanwhile, Herbie and the shiny Lancia accelerate their romance by heading off to quaint spots in the city at the most inopportune moments. Although thieves Max and Quincey chase Herbie relentlessly, they just can't quite nab the car to extract the diamond from the gas tank.

As day of the big race arrives, Herbie is more infatuated with the Lancia than ever. The race to Monte Carlo is loaded with surprises, most of which are launched by the jewel thieves in an effort to seize Herbie once and for all. All seems desperately lost when Herbie is forced to climb a rugged mountaintop. But the trusty Volkswagon shifts gears and narrowly escapes with Wheely and Jim in near hysterics. Despite all the close calls, Jim and Wheely do their best to stay in the race and stay alive. As expected, Herbie zooms across the finish line in Monte Carlo to win the Trans-France. Herbie saves the day by thwarting the efforts of the jewel thieves all by himself. So all ends well. In the romantic city of Monte Carlo, Jim and Diane fall in love, Wheely finds an attractive companion, and Herbie resumes his romance with the bewitching Lancia—whose name turns out to be Giselle.

Wheely and Jim discover the precious stolen diamond hidden in Herbie's gas tank.

Sidelights

- When the film premiered, Herbie, Don Knotts, and Dean Jones were on hand at Mann's Chinese Theatre in Hollywood to place Herbie's tire prints in cement. (The tire prints are no longer there.)
- Some of the movie was filmed on location in Paris, France; the French Riviera; and of course, Monte Carlo.

Herbie the love bug falls in love while in Europe.

ABOVE: Racing becomes a dangerous sport when Herbie is led up a steep mountain. LEFT: Mechanic Wheely Applegate (Knotts) is no match for the hefty diamond thief (Roy Kinnear).

- Herbie is a 1963 white Volkswagen Beetle deluxe ragtop sedan painted in Volkswagen L87 pearl white, with a souped-up motor, racing stripes, and Number 53 on its hood. Herbie's first film adventure was *The Love Bug,* produced by Walt Disney Productions, which earned the popular auto a worldwide fan following and became the top moneymaking film of 1969. So successful, it prompted a sequel five years later, *Herbie Rides Again.* More from the film franchise followed with *Herbie Goes Bananas* in 1980 and *Herbie Fully Loaded* in 2005.

Reviews

Leonard Maltin's Movie Video Guide: "Disney's *Love Bug* formula is starting to run out of gas."

HOT LEAD AND COLD FEET

Released: 1978
Produced by: Ron Miller
Written by: Arthur Alsberg, Joseph McEveety, Don Nelson,
Rod Piffath
Directed by: Robert Butler
Running Time: 90 minutes
Walt Disney Productions

Cast

Jim Dale (Eli Bloodshy/Wild Billy Bloodshy/Jasper Bloodshy), Karen Valentine (Jenny Willingham), Don Knotts (Sheriff Denver Kid), Jack Elam (Rattlesnake), John Williams (Mansfield), Warren Vanders (Boss Snead), Debbie Lytton (Roxanne), Michael Sharrett (Marcus), David S. Cass Sr. (Jack), Richard Wright (Pete), Don "Red" Barry (Bartender), James Van Patten (Jake), Gregg Palmer (Jeff), Ed Bakey (Joshua), John Steadman (Old Codger), Jack Bender (Farmer #3), Norland Benson (Farmer #1), Don Brodie (Saloon Man #3), Art Burke (Official #4), Stanley Clements (Saloon Man #2), Warde Donovan (Saloon Man #4), Russ Fast (Official #2), Ron Honthaner (Saloon Man #5), Mike Howden (Official #3), Hap Lawrence (Cowboy #3), Paul Lukather (Cowboy #2), Dal McKennon (Saloon Man #1), James Michaelford (Dead-Eye), Terry Nicholas, Robert Rothwell (Cowboy #4), Eric Server (Cowboy #1), Brad Weston (Indian), Jim Whitecloud (Indian Chief)

Synopsis

In the old Western town of Bloodshy, Jasper Bloodshy, a rickety old cowboy who founded the town, informs his trusted valet, Mansfield, that he is going to leave all of his wealth to his two sons, Wild Billy Bloodshy, a mean cuss feared by the whole town; and Eli, a long-lost son he has just discovered. Soon, Jasper Bloodshy is involved in an apparent accident and presumed dead. However, Jasper has in fact faked his own death in an attempt to lead his two sons into a competition for the inheritance.

Old man Bloodshy's will is read by the crooked Mayor Ragsdale. Wild Billy Bloodshy is surprised to discover the existence of Eli, a brother he never knew he had. Eli, a kind and God-fearing man, travels from Philadelphia to the town of Bloodshy with two orphans, Roxanne, age eleven, and Marcus, age twelve. When he arrives, he discovers he is just the opposite of his look-alike brother. The two siblings are required by the will to compete against each other in a series of physical races in order to claim the inheritance.

Meanwhile, the Denver Kid, deputy sheriff of the mean and mangy frontier town, rumbles constantly with a worn-out gunslinger named Rattlesnake. The two carry on a feud that ends with no winners.

The race for the inheritance proves to be an exhaustive adventure for both Bloodshy brothers. They fight the rapids in canoes, dodge rocks and boulders, and scale a mountain to the finish. A gang of three gunslingers hired by the corrupt mayor try to make sure that both Eli *and* Wild Billy finish dead last—and dead themselves. That plot is spoiled by none other than old man Jasper, who has been spying on the boys throughout the entire competition.

Mayor Ragsdale's plot to claim the inheritance himself is unveiled to all the townsfolk, and the brothers join forces to rid the town of the crooked politician and clean up the town once and for all.

Don Knotts was essentially playing Barney Fife in the Old West in the film *Hot Lead and Cold Feet.*

Sidelights

- The Los Angeles premiere was held on August 9, 1978.
- The original title for this film was *Bloodshy.*
- Much of the principal photography was shot near Bend, Oregon.
- Stunts were coordinated by Buddy Joe Hooker.
- While Don Knotts and Jack Elam are both given star billing, they

have relatively little to do in this film. Don Knotts's role is not a major one, but essentially the comedian is playing an Old West version of Barney Fife; he makes the best of his screen time with eyes bugged and tempers rising. Knotts and Jack Elam, another great set of Hollywood "eyes," end up carrying out some very funny competitive gags throughout the film.

Reviews

Los Angeles Times: "*Hot Lead and Cold Feet* is more robust than most, with enough stunt action to deck out three ordinary westerns. . . . Not a drop of blood is shed, of course, and when the mud dries and the dust settles, the familiar elements are there as ever they were. . . . In a running gag of a subplot, Don Knotts as the sheriff and Jack Elam as an outlaw keep counting down for a shoot-out, which is always interrupted by a saving calamity like quicksand or a collapsing building. It's little to do, done very entertainingly."

Hollywood Reporter: "Mack Sennett would have loved *Hot Lead and Cold Feet,* a new Disney release for summer ticket-buyers which is practically wall-to-wall slapstick. Actors (and stunt players) fall on their faces, plop into mud pools, tumble out of windows and wagons, get trapped on runaway steam engines, jump off mountain ledges, get knocked off roofs, bounce down river rapids, somersault into horse troughs, get tangled with runaway horses—anything for the sake of a gag or a guffaw."

Variety: "Through years of cinematic conditioning, the Walt Disney organization has groomed its audience to expect the predictable: a clean, fun type of picture that will not embarrass any member of the audience and may even amuse the folks, as well as the toddlers. Always doing the predictable leads to a rut, however, and *Hot Lead and Cold Feet* is mired in just such a groove; outlook is spotty. . . . Antiseptic enough to pass hospital muster, it lampoons a genre most moppets aren't even aware of. For a generation growing up on *Star Trek* and *Star Wars,* the humor in *Hot Lead* is about as potent as the blank bullets being fired every other moment on screen."

THE APPLE DUMPLING GANG RIDES AGAIN

Released: 1979
Produced by: Ron Miller
Written by: Don Tait
Directed by: Vincent McEveety
Running Time: 88 minutes
Walt Disney Productions

Cast

Don Knotts (Theodore Ogelvie), Tim Conway (Amos Tucker), Tim Matheson (Pvt. Jeff Reid), Kenneth Mars (Marshal Wooly Bill Hitchcock), Elyssa Davalos (Milly Gaskill), Jack Elam (Big Mac), Robert Pine (Lt. Jim Ravencroft), Harry Morgan (Major Gaskill), Ruth Buzzi (Old Tough Kate "Granny"), Audrey Totter (Martha Osten), Richard X. Slattery (Sgt. Slaughter), John Crawford (Sherick), Cliff Osmond (Wes Hardin), Ted Gehring (Frank Starrett), Morgan Paull (Corporal #1), Robert Totten (Blainey), James Almanzar (Lennie), Shug Fisher (Bartender), Rex Holman (Reno), Roger Mobley (Sentry #1), Ralph Manza (Little Guy), Stu Gilliam (Cook), A. J. Bakunas (Henchman #1), David S. Cass Sr. (Henchman #2), Louie Elias (Henchman #3), James Van Patten (Soldier #1), Jay Ripley (Soldier #2), Nick Ramus (Indian Chief), George Chandler (Elderly Man at Police Office), Bryan O'Byrne (Photographer), Jack Perkins (Junction City Drunk), John Wheeler (Conductor), Art Evans (Baggage Master), Ed McCready (Citizen #1), Ted Jordan (Citizen #2), Peter Renaday (Jailer at Fort), Bobby Rolofson (Boy), Tom Jackman (Officer #1), Joe Baker (Prisoner Joe), Allan Studley (Prisoner Pete), Michael Masters (Cowboy), John Arndt (Cavalry Man #1), Bill Erickson (Cavalry Man #2), Vince Deadrick Jr. (Sentry #2), Gary McLarty (Corporal #2), Bill Hart (Officer #2), Mickey Gilbert (Tough Guy #1), Wally Brooks, Stacy Elias, Mike Elias (Stunt Performers), Jessica Biscardi

Synopsis

A sequel to *The Apple Dumpling Gang,* the story takes up where we last saw inept outlaws Amos and Theodore. The well-worn outlaws ride into Junction City to deposit their savings in the local bank,

unaware that it is being robbed by Frank Starrett and his sidekick, Wes Hardin. Starrett escapes with Amos and Theodore's donkey, Clarise, which is carrying the money bags. Amos and Theodore are left behind looking guilty. Townswoman Tough Kate encourages local legendary lawman Woolly Bill Hitchcock to handle the punishment. Eventually, Clarise leaves her captors and rejoins Amos and Theodore with the money still strapped to her back. After an unsuccessful attempt to return the bank's money, Amos and Theodore flee the town.

Determined to track down the thieves, Woolly Bill Hitchcock trails the donkey. Arriving at Fort Concho, Amos and Theodore are quickly recruited into the cavalry. Soon, by way of their inept actions bungling a party at the fort, they turn the place upside down and nearly burn the entire camp down. Meanwhile, a court-martial finds Amos and Theodore guilty, and they are sent to Bridger Military Prison. While in prison, the pair stumble across an underground conference room and the sumptuous living quarters of outlaw Big Mac and his gang—the culprits responsible for the Fort Concho raids. Amos and Theodore convince Big Mac to take them on as partners in crime, but in fact the duo plans to thwart the next mission and become heroes. When the sun finally sets, the pair ride off into the sagebrush as free men, cleared of all charges.

Sidelights

- The original title of this film was *Trail's End.*
- The Los Angeles premiere was held on July 11, 1979.
- Fort Kanab, Utah (an original fort from 1864 to 1866), was the setting for much of the action. Shooting in 110-degree heat, the cast melted in their boots.
- The train setting was shot in Sonora, California.
- Critic Robert Osborne (seen as a host on Turner Classic Movies), was not very kind to Tim Conway's performance in his review.

He wrote: "Knotts, as usual, is extremely funny, always incorporating some truth into his comedy, even when slapsticking. Conway is less successful since he overplays the schtick, leaving the impression he thinks he's far more hilarious than he really is. Doing less would have served him better."

Reviews

New York Times: "Walt Disney's *The Apple Dumpling Gang Rides Again* is a sequel of sorts to the company's 1975 comedy about some incredibly lovable moppets, a card sharp and two inept bandits, played by Don Knotts and Tim Conway. . . . The veteran actor Harry Morgan has some nice moments as the commandant of a frontier fort that Mr. Knotts and Mr. Conway accidentally burn down as they are attempting to serve fruit punch."

Los Angeles Herald-Examiner: "*The Apple Dumpling Gang Rides Again* is a Western— very much a Disney Western—and even the dust raised by the horses' hooves look fake. There's some peripheral good humor in the buddy-buddy bungling of Knotts and Conway. . . . They accidentally hold up a bank and then go undercover as Army recruits, but most of it makes *Hee Haw* seem like Noel Coward."

Hollywood Reporter: "It's a spunky cartoon (of the non-animated variety) which should tickle the nippers and entertain mom and pop as well. . . . The only thing missing is moppets. It's unusual (but refreshing) for a Disney picture that there's no one in camera range who hasn't reached puberty."

ABOVE: Sergeant Slaughter (Richard X. Slattery) goes berserk trying to train these new recruits. RIGHT: Theodore and Amos dress in drag to elude bank robbers in *The Apple Dumpling Gang Rides Again*. BELOW: The deft duo are punished for burning the fort down.

THE PRIZE FIGHTER

Released: 1979
Produced by: Wanda Dell, Lang Elliott
Written by: Tim Conway, John Myhers
Directed by: Michael Preece
Running Time: 99 minutes
New World Pictures

Cast

Tim Conway (Bags), Don Knotts (Shakes), David Wayne (Pops Morgan), Cisse Cameron (Polly), Robin Clarke (Mike), Holly Conover (Judy), Bill Ash (Towel Man), Alfred E. Covington (Ring Announcer), Bill Crabb (Turk), Kenneth Daniel (Stubby), Mike DeFais (Referee #2), Joe Dorsey (Stranger), J. Don Ferguson (Referee #1), Dan Fitzgerald (Big John), Charles Franzen (Reporter #1), Les Hatfield (Champ), Ted Henning (Jimmy), Charles R. Honce Jr. (Dale), Edith Ivey (Tough Lady), Billy J. Johnson (Photo Man), Bryan Jones (Andy), May Keller (Lilly), Irwin Keyes (Flower), Joan Benedict (Dori), Michael LaGuardia (Butcher), John Myhers (Doyle), Danny Nelson (Guesser), George Nutting (Timmy), Scott Oliver (Barker), Mary Ellen O'Neill (Mama), Marc Pickard (Reporter #2), Johnny Popwell Sr. (Grader), Fred Saxon (Radio Announcer), Howard Stopeck (Cook), Roy Tatum (Nails), Lou Walker (Janitor), Merle G. Cain (Bumper), Geoff Webber (Bradshaw), Wallace K. Wilkinson (Flash), Willie J. Woods (Spider), Jimmy Cook (Boxer), Perry Quinn (Boxer), Jerry Campbell (Boxer), Clyde Jones (Boxer), Richard Haliburton (Boxer), Aron Siegel (Carnival Attendee)

Synopsis

In the 1930s, two pals—a down-and-out boxer named Bags and his trainer, Shake—get mixed up with mobsters and fixing fights. When the trainer befriends a gangster involved in the fight game, they unknowingly agree to a series of fixed matches. Not realizing that his victories were all setups, Bags accepts a bout with the defending champ, "The Butcher," ending with a hilarious showdown for the heavyweight championship of the world.

Sidelights

- The film was completed in June 1979. The site of filming was in Atlanta, Georgia, at the home of Mr. and Mrs. Reuben Garland. The mansion is an exact copy of the famous deMedici Palace located in Florence, Italy.

Tim Conway, who actually boxed in his younger years, says this was his favorite film to team with Don Knotts.

- Watch for the movie's writer, John Myhers, as "Doyle."
- In an unusual bit, Knotts and Conway perform a cute duet called "Till the End."
- *The Prize Fighter* was a Christmas 1979 film; it earned an opening weekend domestic box-office gross of $822,000 (in 234 theaters in the southern states).

Reviews

Los Angeles Herald-Examiner: "The combination of Don Knotts and Tim Conway in a fight film take off suggests, at the very least, a few pleasant moments of high-energy low comedy, but *The Prize Fighter* can't seem to manage any. This limp little comedy goes down for the count long before it gets a chance to throw a punch. . . . Here, Conway and Knotts not only don't try anything new, they don't even do the sort of work that brought them success to begin with."

Hollywood Reporter: "In their third picture together, Don Knotts and

Tim Conway are getting
more and more like Abbott
& Costello, but unfortu-
nately not as good. Still,
the two comics have talent,
and more importantly, a
strong following in the hin-
terlands, where *The Prize
Fighter* has already played
to respectable business. . . .
What the pair need here is
a script. The lame, pre-
dictable hackneyed mess
cooked up by Conway and
John Myhers leaves them
with nothing but schtick
and aged sight gags, up to
and including crashing into
a chicken truck."

Don Knotts manages Tim
Conway's boxing career in
The Prize Fighter.

THE PRIVATE EYES

Released: 1981
Produced by: Wanda Dell, Lang Elliott
Written by: Tim Conway, John Myhers
Directed by: Lang Elliott
Running Time: 91 minutes
New World Pictures

Cast

Tim Conway (Dr. Tart), Don Knotts (Inspector Winship), Trisha Noble (Mistress Phyllis Morley), Bernard Fox (Justin), Grace Zabriskie (Nanny), John Fujioka (Mr. Uwatsum), Stan Ross (Tibet), Irwin Keyes (Jock), Suzy Mandel (Hilda), Fred Stuthman (Lord Morley), Mary Nell Santacroce (Lady Morley), Robert V. Barron (Gas Station Attendant), Patrick Cranshaw (Roy), Russi Taylor (Doll's Voice)

Synopsis

Lord and Lady Morley have been murdered one foggy night. And what's worse, the inept team of Inspector Winship and Dr. Tart are on the case. Dispatched to investigate, Tart and Winship attempt to figure out which member of the suspected mansion staff is the killer. Is it the butler, the maid, or the mute gardner? Surprisingly, they also receive a letter from Morley *after* he is dead.

At the Morley mansion, the private eyes gather the staff, including a bimbo maid, a gypsy caretaker, a hunchbacked stable groom, a nutty butler, and a seductive mistress. A wasteful interrogation takes place, with no clues to go on. One of these people is the killer . . . but who? Tart and Winship continue to piece together the mystery by questioning the staff, but as the night wears, the bodies start piling up one by one as staff members are picked off by a mysterious shadow lurking in the dark.

Time begins to run out as the two men bumble and stumble their way through the dark reaches of the house and hidden rooms, searching for clues in the form of wacky notes and poems left behind by the killer. But will they find the fiend in time, or will Tart, Winship, and the rest of the manor end up as yesterday's leftovers?

> " Maybe ya gotta try to throw up? You know what my mother used to say to make you throw up? Drink a glass of warm milk with lard in it. Chunks and all. You ever have pudding with cat hair in it? "
>
> —Dr. Tart (Tim Conway)

Dr. Tart and Inspector Winship examine the facts in *The Private Eyes.*

Sidelights

- The wacky clues, given in the form of brief limericks, go way beyond the point of being funny somewhere about midway through the film. Here's one particular gem:

    "If Jock could talk, he'd give you a clue
    Now that he's dead, what can you do?
    He deserved what he got, I don't regret it a bit.
    By the way, you're standing in bull caca."

- Surprisingly, *Private Eyes* did a highly respectable business at the box office, earning the spot as one of the largest grossing independent films of 1980–81. The film reportedly earned more than $15 million in its initial engagement.

- Much of the film was shot at the famous Biltmore House mansion and gardens in Asheville, North Carolina. The Biltmore House was also the location for the 1979 film *Being There* starring Peter Sellers and Shirley MacLaine.

- This is not to be mistaken for the old Bowery Boys movie of the same name, starring Leo Gorcey and Huntz Hall, released in 1953.

The team follows some warped clues to find a murderer.

- Don Knotts told the press during publicity chores for the film that he was not actively seeking a "comedy partner," but as long as it was Tim Conway, he was all for it. "I think Tim may be one of the funniest men in the world. It's difficult to explain why we work so well together. Even the fact that we have a mutual admiration society doesn't entirely explain it. Maybe it's because he makes me laugh when I work with him. I put myself in the straight-man position when we're in a scene together. I consider him the zany one. I'm like Hardy to his Laurel. I enjoy that relationship with him."

Reviews

Los Angeles Herald-Examiner: "With his strangled voice and prune-faced winces Don Knotts, when put in the right context, is a reliable, if bizarre, comic character actor. But he can't reach that level in tandem with Conway. A mass of ticks and jerks, Conway is fast looming as the great 'fake-out' artist of contemporary comedians. He always seems to be on the verge of doing something 'brilliant.' The fact is, he never manages to do so. He just sets up a distracting flurry of movements which cover his tracks so well you begin to suspect he has done something you just haven't been clever enough to catch."

Evening Outlook: "There are hunchback jokes in this movie. There are cleft palate jokes. There are jokes about getting barnyard animal excrement on your shoes. There are a lot of running jokes in *The Private Eyes.* But most of them sort of meander like Butterfly

Private eyes . . . are watching you.

McQueen in *Gone With the Wind,* arriving belatedly and out of breath at their destinations without a clue about what they started out to do. You want to slap somebody . . . *The Private Eyes* is an imitation mystery thriller with illusions of grandeur. . . . [The film] contains even less suspense than humor. You can figure out who the killer is in about two seconds flat. Then your only problem is figuring out how to survive the rest of the movie."

CANNONBALL RUN II

Released: 1984
Produced by: Albert S. Ruddy
Written by: Brock Yates, Hal Needham, Albert S. Ruddy,
Harvey Miller
Directed by: Hal Needham
Running Time: 108 minutes
Warner Bros.

Cast

Burt Reynolds (J. J. McClure), Dom Deluise (Victor Prinzim/Captain Chaos/Don Canneloni), Dean Martin (Jamie Blake), Sammy Davis Jr. (Morris Fenderbaum), Jamie Farr (The Sheik), Marilu Henner (Betty), Telly Savalas (Hymie Kaplan), Shirley MacLaine (Veronica), Susan Anton (Jill), Catherine Bach (Marcie), Foster Brooks (Fisherman), Sid Caesar (Fisherman), Jackie Chan (Himself), Tim Conway (CHP Officer), Tony Danza (Terry), Jack Elam (Dr. Nikolas Van Helsing), Michael V. Gazzo (Sonny), Richard Kiel (Arnold), Don Knotts (CHP Officer), Richardo Montalban (King), Jim Nabors (Pvt. Homer Lyle), Louis Nye (Fisherman), Molly Picon (Mrs. Goldfarb), Charles Nelson Reilly (Don Don Canneloni), Alex Rocco (Tony), Henry Silva (Slim), Frank Sinatra (Himself), Joe Theismann (Mack), Mel Tillis (Mel), Abe Vigoda (Caesar), Fred Dryer (Sergeant CHP), Dale Ishimoto (Japanese Businessman), Arte Johnson (Pilot), Linda Lei (Beautiful Girl), Chris Lemmon (Young CHP Officer), George Lindsey (Uncle Cal), Doug McClure (The Slapper), Jilly Rizzo (Jilly), Dub Taylor (Sheriff), Shawn Weatherly (Blake's Girl), Sean Alexander (Gas Station Attendant), Beatrice Dunmore (Talkative Noisy Spectator), Debi Greco (Sheik's Girl), Sandy Hackett (Official), Lee Kolima (Nicky), Cheech Marin (Tire Store Employee), Fred S. Ronnow (Pilot), Bob Sheldon (Policeman at Lake), Jack Smith (Announcer), Sean Stanek (Gas Station Attendant), John Worthington Stuart (Bartender), Frank Welker Special Voice Effects), Kai J. Wong (Japanese Executive), John A. Zee (Sheldon), Marty Allen, Jim Cassett Ander-

Two Too Many Toupees
Don says hello to *Cannonball Run II* star Burt Reynolds at a film premiere.

son, Janet Blair, Patricia Bolt, Beverly Budinger, Robert B. Chandler, Harry P. Gant, Alan Gibbs, Beth Glenn, Suzynn Herzog, Frank O. Hill, Marian Issacks, James C. Lewis, Red McIlvaine (Drivers for Girls), Hal Needham (Porsche 928 Driver with Cowboy Hat), Regina Parton, Caroline Reed, Branscombe Richmond (Bikers), Mario Roberts, Raphael Salcido, Avery Schreiber, Kathleen M. Shea, Frieda Smith, Bud Stout, Bobby Berosini's Orangutan

Synopsis

A sequel to *Cannonball Run,* this story follows J. J. McClure and his sidekick pal, Victor, as the pair of zany cannonballers compete to win a $1 million pot, which Sheik Abdul Ben Falafel has put up as a prize. Careening across country from Redondo Beach, California, to Darien, Connecticut, in a maverick road race, the pair is pitted against numerous oddballs, including a couple of bogus cops, tipsy fishermen, a giant, old-time mafia men, sexy femme fatales, and even karate commandos. When J. J. and Victor give a lift to two phony nuns, the trip becomes a joyride. And of course, an orangutan—serving as a limousine chauffeur for a couple of loons, steals the show. It's full speed ahead as the story takes McClure and Victor through the states as they avoid the police around every turn.

Sidelights

- The film opened on June 29, 1984, in Los Angeles at Mann's Westwood Theatre.
- Filming was done entirely on location in Tucson, Arizona.
- Producer Albert Ruddy, who gave us *The Godfather,* had a part in the Mafioso subplot/satire, even including some of the original cast members from *The Godfather* (Alex Rocco, Abe Vigoda, Michael Gazzo).
- The same orangutan appearing in this film also appeared in *Going Ape.*
- When the two police officers (Don Knotts and Tim Conway) pull over the ape driving the limousine, the ape slaps one of the officers in the head. His head knocks the other officer and they both drop to the ground. Look closely and you will see that their heads never actually touch.
- This marks the final film appearance for Rat Pack veterans together: Frank Sinatra, Dean Martin, and Sammy Davis Jr. (It also marked Sinatra's and Martin's final motion picture appearances in their individual careers.) Along with Shirley MacLaine in the cast, this was officially an unprecedented "Rat Pack" reunion.

- The theme song, "Like a Cannonball," was sung by the musical boy band Menudo, featuring a very young Ricky Martin.

Reviews

Los Angeles Times: "If you bother to submit yourself to *Cannonball Run II* and happen to go the distance, be sure to stay for the end credits, the funniest part of the picture by far. As they unroll on the left of the screen, we're treated to a series of bloopers showing the stars breaking each other up during shooting, blowing one take after another . . . ah, if only this antic humor had been allowed to burst through earlier."

Hollywood Reporter: "There are, to be sure, moments and sequences of inspired lunacy. Don Knotts and Tim Conway, as a couple of highway patrolmen who try to ticket an orangutan, are undeniably hilarious. Conway is convinced the orangutan is really Allen Funt in disguise and that the whole episode is a *Candid Camera* setup."

Los Angeles Herald-Examiner: "The film even skimps on the usual car chases and demolition wheelies and skidding u-turns; most of the plot is taken up with dumb-dumb routines involving the Rat Pack and a gaggle of cartoon Mafiosi, Arabs, fake cops, jump-suited Amazons, tipsy fishermen, kung fu cutups, giants, and truckers. Hal Needham's direction is so incompetent that, at the end, you're not even sure who won the race."

RETURN TO MAYBERRY

Broadcast April 14, 1986
Produced by: Richard O. Linke, Dean Hargrove
Written by: Harvey Bullock, Everett Greenbaum
Directed by: Bob Sweeney
Running Time: 95 minutes
NBC-TV

Cast

Andy Griffith (Andy Taylor), Ron Howard (Opie Taylor), Don Knotts (Barney Fife), George Lindsey (Goober Pyle), Jim Nabors (Gomer Pyle), Betty Lynn (Thelma Lou), Aneta Corsaut (Helen Crump Taylor), Howard Morris (Ernest T. Bass), Jack Dodson (Howard Sprague), Maggie Peterson (Charlene Darling), Denver Pyle (Briscoe Darling), Hal Smith (Otis Campbell), Robert Broyles (Wilson), Karlene Crockett (Eunice Taylor), Rance Howard (Preacher), Karen Knotts (Newspaper Receptionist), Richard Lineback (Wally Butler), Allen Williams (Lloyd Fox), Paul Wilson (Ben Woods), Janet Waldo (Voice of Aunt Bee). As the Darlings: Doug Dillard, Rodney Dillard, Mitch Jayne, and Dean Webb

Synopsis

Lovable Andy Taylor has been away from Mayberry, North Carolina, for twenty years, living in Cleveland and working as a U.S. Postal Service inspector. He and his wife, Helen, return home (mysteriously without his second-born son, Andy Jr., christened on *Mayberry R.F.D.*). Andy's main purpose for returning is to see son Opie, as he is now about to become a father.

Andy discovers that his old deputy and cousin, Barney Fife, has returned from Raleigh and is now the acting sheriff following the death of the preceding sheriff. Barney intends to run for sheriff in the town's upcoming political race. (Weren't Andy and Barney keeping in touch over the decades? How sad.) Barney becomes annoyed as many townspeople assume that Andy has returned to assume the sheriff's position (despite Andy's constant denial) and beg him to run for office. Meanwhile, Barney becomes involved in a kooky commercial ploy to attract tourists to the area: the sighting of a mysterious monster in Myer's Lake.

Opie, now the town's newspaper publisher, ponders moving his family out of Mayberry to expand his journalism career and vacate small-town life. Eventually, when Opie's wife goes into labor and Andy can't get his daughter-in-law to the hospital in time, the former sheriff confidently delivers his own grandchild right there in the back of the automobile.

Many familiar residents of Mayberry are revisited. The boring Howard Sprague attempts to regain his youth by making the painful decision to dye his hair. Howard is now working as a staff photographer for the local newspaper. Cousins Gomer and Goober Pyle, still inept as ever, are now co-owners of the town's main filling station and auto repair center. Briscoe Darling and his hillbilly clan, including wacky Ernest T. Bass, come down from the mountain to greet the sheriff upon his return. Otis Campbell, the former town drunk, has been sober for years and drives an ice-cream truck. Thelma Lou returns to Mayberry and learns that Barney is still unmarried and seeks to reunite with her old boyfriend after all these years.

In the end, Andy discovers that local hotel owner Wally Butler hired Ernest T. Bass to propagate the lake monster panic. (A dragon artifact was confiscated from a defunct Chinese restaurant in a nearby town and used to appear like a lake monster.) At a "victory rally" for Barney, an informal straw poll is taken and Andy is favored as sheriff despite not being on the ballot. In order to allow Barney to

The Mayberry gang reunite in the 1986 TV movie *Return to Mayberry*: Jim Nabors, George Lindsay, Don Knotts, Andy Griffith, and Ron Howard.

realize his dream, Andy refuses to enter the race. Surprisingly, Barney turns everything upside down and makes an emotional withdrawal speech as he publicly endorses his old pal, "Ange." Andy finally agrees to serve. The final shot of the film is the "new" sheriff and deputy raising an American flag on Mayberry's Main Street flagpole . . . just like the old days.

Sidelights/Behind the Scenes

- The TV special was filmed in the Southern California town of Los Olivos, with existing buildings in the town square doubling for modern-day Mayberry.
- This is one of the few times that cousins Gomer (Jim Nabors) and

Goober (George Lindsay) actually appear together in a Mayberry script.

- Don Knotts's daughter, Karen, portrays a secretary at the town's newspaper office.
- Watch for many references to the original series, *The Andy Griffith Show*: Barney serenades "Juanita" on the old candlestick telephone; Andy refers to the bird incident; Andy and Opie reflect on the old days (the show's opening), when father and son strolled the lakeside and Opie threw rocks into Myer's Lake; Barney pulls a single bullet from his shirt pocket; at a restaurant, Barney and Andy recall the Fun Girls from Mount Pilot; the Darlings and Andy perform a new version of "Dooley."
- The feeling of the TV movie is very laid-back, reminiscent of Mayberry, but the tone is a bit strange without a laugh track. It almost has the feel of an episode of *The Waltons* rather than *The Andy Griffith Show*.
- Watch for Ron Howard's father, Rance, playing the preacher.
- Ron Howard celebrated his thirty-second birthday on the set of the movie with a large decorated sheet cake; on hand were Andy Griffith, Jim Nabors, George Lindsey, and other cast members gathered around, closely cheering him on.
- Child actor Clint Howard, the younger brother of Ron, was offered the role of Wally Butler (which was eventually played by Richard Lineback). Clint Howard had appeared as young Leon—toting the ever-present peanut butter and jelly sandwich—on the

Return to Mayberry reunited a whole bevy of old friends from *The Andy Griffith Show*. The TV movie aired on NBC in 1986 and won fantastic ratings.

original *Andy Griffith Show.* Howard had to decline the offer of a role in *Return to Mayberry* because he was in Tucson working on a film called *The Wraith* with Randy Quaid and Charlie Sheen.

- The local Mayberry paper was now the *Courier Express,* with Opie working as the editor. It was named the *Courier Express* because writer Everett Green-baum's hometown newspaper in Buffalo, New York, had the same name. Greenbaum also used the Buffalo newspaper in *The Ghost and Mr. Chicken,* in which Luther Heggs was employed by the *Rachel Courier Express.* Green-baum told writer Jim Clark that he and veteran Mayberry writer Har-vey Bullock took over the *Return to Mayberry* script after several other writers failed to come up with a story that Andy Griffith found appropriate. Regarding the reunion movie, Greenbaum added, "It was as though the years had just slipped away. I had been see-ing Andy and Don through the years, but we wanted to see as many of the people from the old show as we could. And of course, we had to get Barney and Thelma Lou back together."

- Actress Frances Bavier, who por-trayed Aunt Bee, was living in Siler City, North Carolina. She was retired, age eighty-four at the time,

Andy returns to Mayberry to resume his job as sheriff, only to find out Barney is running for the position.

and living there in fair health with several cats. When she was offered a role in the TV movie she declined. Her role was then reduced and only off-camera lines were written; the production asked if she would just record the lines for the film's opening, but she again declined and said she preferred not to participate. According to Ron Howard, who flew out and met with Bavier briefly, she did not want to reminisce about the old days or have anything to do with the movie. (She even admonished the former child actor and costar for simply showing up at her home.) Hard feelings between her and Andy Griffith remained; they were not particularly friendly during the original series. (Bavier died a few

Howard Morris

Although he is best known for his portrayal of the irascible Ernest T. Bass on *The Andy Griffith Show*, fans may be surprised to discover that Howard Morris was also a talented director, classically trained Shakespearean actor, and one of Hollywood's most prolific voiceover artists.

Born in the Bronx, Morris got his start acting in New York, where he earned a scholarship in dramatic arts from New York University. After serving in the army during World War II, he returned to New York and landed a spot as a sketch comedian on Sid Caesar's popular *Your Show of Shows*. Later making the move to Hollywood, he guest-starred on *Wanted: Dead or Alive*, *Alfred Hitchcock Presents*, *The Twilight Zone*, *The Dick Van Dyke Show*, and dozens of other television shows. He also played Mr. Elmer Kelp in Jerry Lewis's *The Nutty Professor*.

His first appearance on *Andy Griffith* as "Ernest T. Bass" came in an episode called "The Mountain Wedding," which aired in 1963. Although he initially wondered if a boy from the Bronx could pull off the role of a "Southern cuckoo," Morris came to relish the part. "When I became Ernest T. . . . my insides would warm with joy," he later said. "They gave me a lot of freedom with that character. I invented all the rhyming."

Behind the scenes, Howard Morris began making a name for himself as a Hollywood director. In addition to several episodes of *The Andy Griffith Show*, his directing credits included *Get Smart*, *Hogan's Heroes*, *Bewitched*, *Loredo*, *The Love Boat*, *Trapper John M.D.*, and many feature films and commercials for major advertisers.

When he wasn't in front of the camera or directing, Morris picked up work as a voice artist behind the microphone. With a beautifully inimitable nasal tone, he created literally hundreds of cartoon voices, including characters such as Beetle Bailey, Atom Ant, Mister Peebles (*Magilla Gorilla*), Jughead (*The Archie Show*), a variety of characters on *The Flintstones*, *The Jetsons*, and *The Groovie Goolies*, and in commercials for McDonald's and Kellogg's.

Besides their work together on *The Andy Griffith Show* and in the TV movie *Return to Mayberry*, Howard Morris and Don Knotts worked together professionally only one other time—as voice artists in a 1993 episode of *Garfield and Friends*. Offscreen, they remained good friends, and in later years they often attended an informal monthly meeting of actors and comedians called "Yarmy's Army" in Hollywood together.

Howard loved playing up his role as "Ernest T." for fans and frequently appeared at nostalgia shows to sign autographs. When asked to sign long Mayberry-related inscriptions on photos, he was known to famously quip, "What? Do you want me to write the Lord's Prayer on the head of a pin?"

Howard Morris passed away May 21, 2005, at the age of eighty-five. His son, David Morris, perhaps summed up his father's career best by saying, "He was . . . one in a million, a true genius, and an entertainment dynamo."

—JOEL RASMUSSEN

Howard Morris.

years later in December 1989.) Aunt Bee's lines for the TV movie were recorded by veteran voice-over actress Janet Waldo.

* Actress Maggie Peterson remembers: "I was shocked when they called us all in to do that movie. I never thought they'd do the movie in the first place because Andy is so picky about material. But for whatever reason, I don't think it came off as well as it was written. It was a terrific screenplay. There were things that weren't quite right. I mean, they made Hal Smith, who was Otis the Drunk in the series, an ice-cream man. Now, he didn't want to do that. He didn't like that because he was so in love with his drunk character as Otis. They had some scenes between Goober and Gomer that were very funny and they cut those. Maybe there were too many threads in the plot to make it all come true. I can see why Andy went for it, but I don't think it played out as good as it could have."

PINOCCHIO AND THE EMPEROR OF THE NIGHT

Animated
Released: 1987
Produced by: Lou Scheimer
Written by: Carlo Collodi
Directed by: Hal Sutherland
Running Time: 87 minutes
Filmation Associates

Cast

Scott Grimes (Pinnocchio), Edward Asner (Scalawag), Tom Bosley (Geppetto), James Earl Jones (Emperor of the Night), Don Knotts (Gee Willikers), Lana Beeson (Twinkle), Linda Gary (Beatrice), Jonathan Harris (Lt. Grumblebee), Rickie Lee Jones (Fairy Godmother), Frank Welker (Igor/Mayor of Bugsburg), William Windom (Puppetino), Liza Minnelli

Synopsis

It's Pinocchio's first birthday. He's been a real boy for a year now, so his creator, Geppetto, makes him a cake to celebrate. After a visit from Pinocchio's fairy godmother (the one who magically transformed the puppet into a real boy), Geppetto decides to deliver a gift—a precious jewel box—to the mayor of Bugsburgh. Pinocchio persuades Geppetto to allow him to deliver the gift personally to the mayor.

Accompanying Pinocchio is his handmade glowworm, which magically becomes real; he names him Willikers. Distracted by the lights and music of a carnival, Pinocchio and Willikers decide to see what all the excitement is about. Nearby, con artists Scalawag and his colleague, Igor, advertise a three-shell game that cheats people out of their money. The pair is discovered and Scalawag and Igor escape by using a cannon to get away from the angry mob.

Scalawag meets Pinocchio

Filmation's *Pinocchio and the Emperor of the Night* pulled Don back into the recording studio for more voiceover work after a ten-year absence.

and trades the jewel box for a fake ruby. When Pinocchio returns home, he finds Geppetto angry. Pinocchio runs away to the carnival, where he watches a performance and falls in love with the star puppet, Twinkle. After the customers have left, the puppet master, Puppetino, explains to Pinnochio about what it takes to be a performer, then transforms him into an evil puppet. With help from Willikers and the fairy godmother, Pinocchio eventually escapes from the carnival and searches for the jewel box. Along the way, he promises his new friend Twinkle that he will find a way to make her real as well.

Pinocchio finds Scalawag and Igor and demands the return of the jewel box. Scalawag tells Pinocchio that he does not have it and says that they were outnumbered by a gang of thieves led by Puppetino, who stole it from them. Pinocchio tracks down the carnival with assistance from Scalawag, who secretly intends to hand him over to Puppetino in exchange for gold. The carnival, however, is a lot more mysterious and evil than it seems . . . including the evil master of the carnival—the Emperor of the Night. It's a magical trip in which Pinocchio finally understands the value of freedom and the meaning of true friendship.

Sidelights

Don Knotts portrays Gee Willikers, the talking glow worm who befriends Pinocchio. Gee Willikers could be considered the equivalent of Jiminy Cricket from the original Disney version of *Pinocchio.*

MATLOCK: THE ASSASSINATION

Broadcast Date: May 8, 1992
Written by: Anne Collins, Joel Steiger, Gerald Sanoff
Directed by: Christopher Hibler
Running Time: 97 minutess
NBC-TV

Cast

Andy Griffith (Matlock), Don Knotts (Les), Daniel Roebuck (ADA Sadowsky), Kristoffer Tabori (Judge Arthur Eller), Rene Auberjonois (Leo Brodsky), Eddie Jones (Chief Colin Young), Neil Giuntoli (Judd Taylor), Jeff Osterhage (Matt Greenwood), Michael Bowen (Jay Reynolds), Alexander Zale (Judge #2), Bretly W. R. Baughn (Jury Foreperson), Michael Cannizzo (Officer), Deborah Wait (Jury Foreperson #2), John Petlock (Curtis Barthelemew), James Tartan (Judge #1), Daniel Trent (Dale Lambert), Barbara Whinney (Hairdresser), Marta Dubois (Ava Brodsky), Burr De Benning (Mayor), Gregory White (PI), Ann Walker (Landlady), Karon Wright (Secretary), Diane Behrens (Ms. Lumax), Casey Peterson, Jason Schombing, David Cromwell, Wayne Grau, Suzanne Keat

Synopsis/Sidelights

- Attorney Ben Matlock and his daughter investigate the murder of the mayor of Atlanta, Georgia. Ben's latest client is somehow involved. Ben and Leanne link the mayor's assassination to a judge charged with sexual assault. Don Knotts was added to the cast for this two-part episode/movie from the sixth season of the popular series. Knotts plays Ben's neighbor pal, Les Calhoun, a modern-day Barney Fife, only much older and slower. Knotts appeared in a total of fifteen episodes of *Matlock* between 1988 and 1992.

- Former *Andy Griffith Show* writer Everett Greenbaum worked on some of the *Matlock* episodes, specifically those featuring Don Knotts as a special guest star. "My main job was to create a part for Don Knotts," he said. Following that assignment, Greenbaum occasionally worked as an actor on the series, sitting on the bench and donning the black robe as cantankerous Judge Katz.

Don joins Andy Griffith, Julie Sommars, and Nancy Stafford on a two part *Matlock* movie in 1988.

B*IG BULLY

Released: 1996
Produced by: Gary Foster, Lee Rich, James G. Robinson
Written by: Mark Steven Johnson
Directed by: Steve Minor
Running Time: 90 minutes
Morgan Creek Productions

Cast

Rick Moranis (David Leary), Tom Arnold (Rosco "Fang" Bigger), Julianne Phillips (Victoria Tucker), Carol Kane (Faith Bigger), Jeffrey Tambor (Art Lundstrum), Curtis Armstrong (Clark), Faith Prince (Betty Lundstrum), Tony Pierce (Ulf), Don Knotts (Principal Kokelar), Blake Bashoff (Ben Leary), Cody McMains (Kirby), Harry Waters Jr. (Alan), Stuart Pankin (Gerry), Justin Jon Ross (Young David), Michael Zwiener (Young Fang), Tiffany Foster (Young Victoria), Matthew Slowick (Young Ulf), C. J. Grayson (Young Alan), Grant Hoover (Young Gerry), Bill Dow (David's Father), Susan Bain (David's Mother), Christine Willes (Grade School Teacher), Ingrid Torrance (4th-Grade Teacher), Tyler Van Blankenstein (Freckle-faced Kid), Doug Abrahams (Guard), Lillian Carlson (Old Woman), Matt Hill (Teenager), Kate Twa (Shop Clerk), Norma MacMillan (Mrs. Rumpert), Eryn Collins (Kid #1), Tegan Moss (Girl in Class), Gregory Smith (Kid #2), Lois Dellar (Teacher #1), Claire Riley (Sympathetic Teacher), Alf Humphreys (Teacher #2), Brent Morrison (Stookie), Alexander Pollock (Corky Bigger), Kyle Labine (Stevie Bigger), Zachary Webb (Kyle Bigger), Eric Pospisil (Bobby Bigger), Miriam Smith (Crying Teacher), Colum Cantillon (Paul), Dawn Stofer-Rupp (Secretary), Steven Taylor (Hallway Kid #1), Justin Goodrich (Hallway Kid #2), Anthony Pavokovic (Hallway Kid #3), Andrew Wheeler (Soldier), James Sherry (Delinquent #1), Tommy Anderson (Delinquent #2), Tina Klassen (Korean Lady), Tamara Stanners (Connie TV Guest), Ray Fairchild (Connie TV Guest), Butch Miller (Wrestler), Brian Wickens (Wrestler)

Synopsis

In the small town of Hastings, Minnesota, lived David Leary, a young boy who is tormented by the school bully: Roscoe Bigger, aka "Fang" (because he has one morbidly sharp cuspid). David is chased after school, picked on, and beat up by Fang on a constant basis. David finally gets his revenge on Fang by ratting him out about stealing a moon rock from a special exhibit. David's parents decide they are moving away from Hastings and David is glad he exposed his nemesis.

Flash-forward several decades. David is now a novelist and a single parent with a son of his own named Ben. David is asked to come teach a semester of creative writing at his old school. He accepts the offer thinking it will be a good change for him and his rebellious son. He returns to Hastings with great optimism and hopes he'll be embraced by the community as a celebrity.

At school, Ben is having trouble adjusting and gets into some trouble for bullying another student named Kirby. David is asked to come to Principal Kokelar's office (the same principal as when he was in school) for a meeting with the boys and Kirby's father, who is the school's current shop teacher. During an apology session after the meeting David realizes Kirby's father is his former nemesis, Roscoe "Fang" Bigger . . . only older, and bigger.

The heat is on as Roscoe gets those old feelings again to antagonize his old pal Davey. Fang goes to work terrorizing David with all types of humiliating and malevolent practical jokes. Eventually, it becomes a daily tormenting session with regular chases and pranks around every corner. Their kids, Kirby and Ben, become friends and finally teach their fathers a lesson about how to get along.

Sidelights

- On the DVD extras, Don Knotts remembers, "Bee Lewis used to chase me home every day. I used to get out of school and run, because he'd always be waiting for me." Director Steve Minor recalls of his youth, "I still have lead in my finger from a kid named Ronnie Egan, who kicked a pencil into my finger in the third grade."
- The character of Ben (Blake Bashoff) makes a sarcastic comment about their small community being like "Mayberry."

Reviews

Los Angeles Times: "Big Bully is the right story in the wrong mold, raising more questions than it is prepared to deal with. Its makers try to shoehorn into the family comedy genre a decidedly dark—and actually quite pertinent—story about the difficulty many American men have in growing up. The material calls for either outright seriousness or pitch-black humor; the result is a waste of a good idea and a good cast."

CATS DON'T DANCE

Animated
Released: 1997
Produced by: Bill Bloom, Timothy Campbell, Paul Gertz,
David Kirschner
Screenplay: Roberts Gannaway, Cliff Ruby, Elana Lesser,
Theresa Pettengill
Story by: Rick Schneider, Robert Lence, Mark Dindal,
Brian McEntee, David Womersley, Kelvin Yasuda
Directed by: Mark Dindal
Running Time: 75 minutes
Warner Bros./Turner Feature Animation

Cast

Scott Bakula (Danny), Jasmine Guy (Sawyer), Natalie Cole (Sawyer Singing Voice), Ashley Peldon (Darla Dimple), Lindsay Ridgeway (Darla Dimple Singing Voice), Kathy Najimy (Tillie Hippo), John Rhys-Davies (Woolie Mammoth), George Kennedy (L. B. Mammoth), Rene Auberjonois (Flanigan), Betty Lou Gerson (Frances), Hal Holbrook (Cranston), Matthew Herried (Pudge the Penguin), Don Knotts (T. W. Turtle), Frank Welker (Farley Wink), David Johansen (Bus Driver), Mark Dindal (Max), Rick Logan (T. W. Turtle Singing Voice)

Synopsis

Picture it: Hollywood, 1939. A talented, ambitious young cat named Danny from Kokomo, Indiana, hops on a bus and comes to Hollywood with a melody in his heart and the dance moves of Fred Astaire in his paws. He's got elaborate dreams of becoming a movie star, finally exposing his talents to the world. When he gets to Tinseltown, he realizes it'll be fancy feast or famine when all he can land are the stereotypical feline roles with "meow" being his sole line. Animal actors just aren't in demand. With his trusted pals, including a discouraged female dancer turned secretary named Sawyer, he sets out to change the studio system single-handedly. Danny falls in love with Sawyer, who encourages him through it all. Things turn sour, however, when Darla Dimple, the famous Mammoth Studios child star, attempts to cleverly ensure that the gang of wannabes will never become a threat to her career. Danny gets on Darla's bad side by stealing a scene with a bit part. In revenge, Darla sics her hulking valet, Max, on Danny and his friends. Danny, with some final inspiration à la *Singin' in the Rain*, exposes Darla for the wicked phony she is.

Sidelights

- L. B. Mammoth is parody of movie mogul Louis B. Mayer. Darla Dimple is named after Darla Hood, one of the cute members of Our Gang/Little Rascals. The "T. W." in T. W. Turtle (voiced by Don Knotts) stands for "Tumble Weed."
- Legendary dancer Gene Kelly served as a mentor on the project, apparently helping with advice on the choreography design not long before his death.

Reviews

New York Times: "While the animated characters, bright colors, and an appealing Randy Newman score may keep the children content, *Cats Don't Dance* is no saccharine fantasy. Its Hollywood references and dark satire constitute its real strengths. . . . There's more than kids' stuff under the plot."

Hollywood Reporter: "Turner Feature Animation dishes out some fancy footwork with *Cats Don't Dance*, a delightful animated musical that conjures up a blend of those all-singin', all-dancin', vintage Hollywood extravaganzas and those deftly satirical Looney Tunes installments of the '30s and '40s."

Roger Ebert/Universal Press Syndicate: "*Cats Don't Dance* is not compelling and it's not a breakthrough, but on its own terms it works well. Whether this will appeal to kids is debatable; the story involves a time and a subject they're not much interested in. But the Randy Newman songs are catchy, the look is bright, the spirits are high, and fans of Hollywood's golden age might find it engaging."

Variety: "Snazzy but old-hat animated feature. Decked out with sharp and colorful design work, some well-drawn characters and six snappy Randy Newman tunes, this first entry from Turner Feature Animation goes down very easily but lacks a hook to make it anything other than a minor kidpic entry commercially."

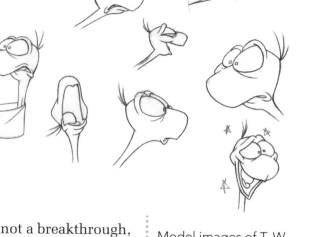

Model images of T. W. Turtle drawn by animator Dave Woodman for *Cats Don't Dance*.

PLEASANTVILLE

Released: 1998
Produced by: Bob Degus, Jon Kilik, Gary Ross, Steven Soderbergh
Written by: Gary Ross
Directed by: Gary Ross
Running Time: 124 minutes
New Line Cinema

Cast

Tobey Maguire (David Parker), Reese Witherspoon (Jennifer Parker), William H. Macy (George Parker), Joan Allen (Betty Parker), Jeff Daniels (Bill Johnson), J. T. Walsh (Big Bob), Don Knotts (TV Repairman), Marley Shelton (Margaret Henderson), Jane Kaczmarek (David's Mom), Giuseppe Andrews (Howard), Jenny Lewis (Christin), Marissa Ribisi (Kimmy), Denise Dowse (Health Teacher), McNally Sagal (Science Teacher), Paul Morgan Stetler (College Counselor), Heather McGill (Girl in School Yard), Kevin Conners (Bud Parker), Natalie Ramsey (Mary Sue Parker), Justin Nimmo (Mark Davis), Kai Lennox (Mark's Lackey #1), Jason Behr (Mark's Lackey #2), Robin Bissell (Commercial Announcer), Harry Singleton (Mr. Simpson), John Ganun (Fireman #1), Paul Walker (Skip Martin), Dawn Cody (Betty Jean), Maggie Lawson (Lisa Anne), Andrea Baker (Peggy Jane), Lela Ivey (Miss Peters), Jim Patric (Tommy), Marc Blucas (Basketball Hero), Stanton Rutledge (Coach), Jason Maves (Paperboy), Gerald Emerick (TV Weatherman), Charles C. Stevenson Jr. (Dr. Henderson), Nancy Lenehan (Marge Jenkins), Weston Blakesley (Gus), Patrick Thomas O'Brien (Roy), Jim Antonio (Ralph), Danny Strong (Jukebox Boy), Kristin Rudrud (Mary), Laura Carney (Bridge Club Lady), Dan Gillies (Fireman #2), Erik MacArthur (Will), Adam Carter (Boy in Soda Shop), David Tom (Whitey), Johnny Moran (Pete), Jeannie Jackson (Woman), J. Patrick Lawlor (Thug), James Keane (Police Chief Dan), Ty Taylor (Thug), Meredith Louise Thomas (Girl in Soda Shop)

Synopsis

David Wagner is a '90s kid with a '50s addiction. He's hooked on reruns of a classic television show called *Pleasantville,* set in a simple place where everyone is swell and perky, "confrontation" is a dirty word, and life is pleasingly pleasant.

Addicted to this utopian world, David immerses himself in *Pleasantville* as an innocent escape from the trouble-plagued real world he must share with his ultrahip, totally popular sister, Jen-

Don plays a mysterious TV repairman who shows Tobey Maguire the way to the past in *Pleasantville*.

nifer. But one evening, life takes a bizarre twist when a peculiar repairman gives him a strange remote control, which zaps David and his sister straight into Pleasantville.

Trapped in a radically different dimension of sight and sound, David and Jennifer find themselves cast as members of the TV family, the Parkers. David has become "Bud" and Jennifer has been transformed into "Mary Sue," and they are surrounded by the black-and-white suburbia that once kept David glued to the television for hours.

It doesn't take long to discover that there's no news, weather, or sports when you're living in a black-and-white paradise where everything is always . . . pleasant. Books have no words, the high school basketball team always wins, and nobody ever questions why things are so perfect. Initially, David revels in the prozac-like haze. But when Jennifer brings her '90s attitude into this unsuspecting era of blandness, things start to happen in living color.

All the repressed desires of life in the '50s begin to boil up through the people of Pleasantville, changing their lives in strange and wonderful ways that none of them had even dared to dream of, until they were visited by two kids from the real world.

Sidelights

Don Knotts's character of a old-fashioned TV repairman is the catalyst for change in this imaginative story. Vaguely sinister, he magically transports the two teenagers into a surreal reality of yesteryear television from the 1950s—life in glorious black and white in the land of bobby sox and dinner promptly at six. Knotts was the carefully chosen TV icon for this film. According to writer/director Gary Ross, there was no other choice. Knotts was the one who added the unique postmodern dimension to the story. So rooted was his beloved Barney Fife character, he represented a bygone television era perfectly for this film.

On the film set, cast members were in awe of Knotts and his presence. Tobey Maguire, the twenty-three-year-old star of the film, told writer Bob Ivry, "Everybody was thrilled that I was working with Don Knotts. I told ten people about the film, that I'm working with

so-and-so, Bill Macy, and Reese Witherspoon and Joan Allen and Don Knotts, and everybody's like, 'Don Knotts! No way! Oh my God! Can I come down to the set when he's working?'"

"I'd always been a big fan," said director Gary Ross, who wrote the script for the huge hit *Big,* starring Tom Hanks, in 1988. "Don's a little bit random and kind of nuts, sort of this evil pixie. He's mercurial, unpredictable. He could go off on a moment's notice. And there's a combustible quality to Don. Remember in the old 'Mayberry' shows, there was that tremendously combustible quality, where we wouldn't know quite what was going to happen, you know, when Barney Fife, would go off. And he's just got chops. What can you say? He can still act so well."

Reviews

TV Guide: "The imaginative and visually dazzling comic fable . . . tempers laughably nostalgic kitsch with a poignant yearning for something more. Imagine June Cleaver realizing that there's life beyond Mayfield, beyond Ward and the boys, and not having a clue about how to respond to this unexpected and unsettling awakening."

Roger Ebert: "*Pleasantville,* which is one of the year's best and most original films, sneaks up on us. It begins by kidding those old black and white sitcoms like *Father Knows Best,* it continues by pretending to be a sitcom itself, and it ends as a social commentary of surprising power. . . . Pleasantville is the kind of parable that encourages us to reevaluate the good old days and take a fresh look at the new world we so easily dismiss as decadent. Yes, we have more problems. But also more solutions, more opportunities and more freedom."

Variety: "*Pleasantville* wouldn't work at all without the extraordinary work of an all-star production team that includes cinematographer John Lindley, production designer Jeannine Oppewall, visual effects supervisor Chris Watts, and perhaps most important, color effects designer Michael Southard. The striking juxtapositions of color and black and white in key scenes are dazzling. But it's the overall persuasiveness of the high tech wizardry that truly elevates Ross's fairy tale above the level of mere gimmickry."

TOM SAWYER

Animated
Released: 2000
Produced by: Jonathan Dern, Paul Sabella
Written by: Patricia Jones, Donald Reiker
Directed by: Phil Mendez, Paul Sabella
Running Time: 89 minutes
MGM Family Entertainment

Cast

Rhett Akins (Tom Sawyer), Mark Wills (Huckleberry Finn), Lee Ann Womack (Becky Thatcher), Hynden Walch (Becky Thatcher), Alecia Elliot (Amy Lawrence), Clea Lewis (Amy Lawrence), Betty White (Aunt Polly), Dean Haglund (Sid), Richard Kind (Mr. Dobbins), Hank Williams Jr. (Injun Joe), Kevin Michael Richardson (Injurin Joe), Don Knotts (Mutt Potter), Waylon Jennings (Judge Thatcher), Dee Bradley Baker (Rebel), Charlie Daniels (Voice)

Synopsis

This unique version of Mark Twain's classic about Tom Sawyer and friends Huck Finn and Becky Thatcher is a musical to delight the entire family. Animated with the characters in the form of furry animals, Tom and Huck get into troubles like skipping school and avoiding their chores. The two constantly daydream about pirates and golden treasure chests and, of course, about Becky Thatcher—the newest little fox at school. When they embark on an adventure, they come across Injun Joe, the town's most grizzly of bears. Injun Joe commits a crime and places the blame on his shaggy pal, Mutt Potter. All the while Huck and Tom witness what Injun Joe has done. Huck and Tom rescue the convicted canine from his undeserving fate and reveal the truth even though they are terrified of the wrath of Injun Joe. Giving Injun Joe the slip, Huck and Tom find themselves in the middle of a fantastic adventure on the mighty Mississippi where mysterious caverns and secret hideouts provide excitement and fortune for the energetic young explorers.

QUINTS

Broadcast Date: August 18, 2000
Produced by: Nicholas Tabarrok
Written by: Matthew Weisman, Gregory K. Pincus
Directed by: Bill Corcoran
Running Time: 83 minutes
A Disney Channel Original Movie

Cast

Jesse Ray Brooks (Commercial Kid), Kimberly J. Brown (Jamie Grover), Tim Burd (Commercial Director), Shawn Campbell (Man in Waiting Room), Vince Corazza (Albert), Cole Corcoran (Adam Grover), Robin Duke (Fiona), Dan Duran (Reporter), Erica Ellis (Hysterical Bridesmaid), Jake Epstein (Brad), Jill Ann Goldhand (Woman in Waiting Room), James Kall (Mr. Blackmer), Don Knotts (Governor Healy), B. J. McQueen (Biker), Elizabeth Morehead (Nancy Grover), Joseph Motiki (Cameraman), Daniel Roebuck (Jim Grover), Shadia Simmons (Zoe)

Synopsis

Young Jamie Grover is a high school student who tells her story about sibling rivalry with a twist. Jamie is an only child, but she

wishes she wasn't always the center of attention. She gets her wish when her parents reveal they are about to have quintuplets. Jamie helps them prepare for the upcoming arrivals. When the celebrated quintuplets are delivered, mayhem quickly engulfs the Grover household, as baby screams constantly echo through the halls and the household is turned upside down. Jamie finds life difficult with the new babies in the house and struggles to assist her parents as the babies become celebrities in the town.

Dan Roebuck on Don Knotts

I worked in the film *Quints* for Disney, and it ended up being Don's final on-camera work. I'd like to say it's a story about a dad who has quintuplets, but I can't. It's about a teenage girl whose parents have quintuplets, and it's from her point of view. I was the dad. The children become famous, and the story involves my young daughter and how she copes.

Don plays the governor of our state, who presents the parents an award. We show up without the kids and the governor really just wanted the photo opportunity with the quintuplets. He's asking, "Where's the babies? I can't believe you didn't bring the babies!" Well, we end up bringing the babies and everything turns out fine.

We shot this in Toronto, but it is supposed to take place in the United States. We rehearsed a little, and I remember he kind of wanted to rehearse. Don was really all about the physicality of where we would be in the room and how we would move. I had to play that I was nervous because he was nervous, but what am I gonna do? I'm working with the king of nervous, so I thought I'd be subtle with my thing . . . because he's Don Knotts and I'm Dan Roebuck.

I actually met Don years before when I was working on *Matlock*. We never had scenes together, but I went down to the set just to meet him and say hi.

I grew up a fan of this stuff; I love old movies and TV, the classics. When you watch *The Andy Griffith Show*, what you can learn about doing comedy in an organic and natural way, you can either write a thousand books about it or you can just shut up and watch. You can never really extrapolate the chemistry.

It's funny how things evolve. When I was a child, I loved *The Incredible Mr. Limpet*. When

you're a kid, any cartoon away from Saturday morning was unique. It's hard for people to remember or believe that, but it was true. Nobody comprehends that now. *The Ghost and Mr. Chicken* is now one of my favorites. It represents everything that was great about that time in my life. It was at Universal Studios; it had those great character actors. It had suspense, silliness, he gets the girl. Maybe we were all feeling a little nerdy when we were kids and getting the girl was a great thing.

I'm blessed in my ridiculous career. I've been in Romulen makeup on the *Star Trek* set and I'm standing there next to Spock. He's got pointy ears and I've got pointy ears. I'm thinking: *I could have never dreamed it.* So, watching *The Andy Griffith Show* as a kid, I could have never dreamed that I'd be standing in Toronto wearing a tuxedo and playing comedy with Don Knotts standing there in a tuxedo. None of these moments are ever taken for granted.

CHICKEN LITTLE

Computer Animated
Released: 2005
Produced by: Randy Fullmer
Written by: Mark Dindal, Mark Kennedy
Directed by: Mark Dindal
Running Time: 81 minutes
Walt Disney Productions

Cast

Zach Braff (Chicken Little), Garry Marshall (Buck Cluck), Don Knotts (Mayor Turkey Lurkey), Patrick Stewart (Mr. Woolensworth), Amy Sedaris (Foxy Loxy), Steve Zahn (Runt of the Litter), Joan Cusack (Abby Mallard), Wallace Shawn (Principal Fetchit), Harry Shearer (Dog Announcer), Fred Willard (Melvin—Alien Dad), Catherine O'Hara (Tina—Alien Mom), Patrick Warburton (Alien Cop), Adam West (Ace—Hollywood Chicken), Mark Walton (Goosey Loosey), Mark Dindal (Morkubine Porcupine/Coach), Dan Molina (Fish Out of Water), Joe Whyte (Rodriguez/Acorn Mascot/Umpire), Sean Elmore (Kirby—Alien Kid), Evan Dunn (Kirby—Alien Kid), Matthew Josten (Kirby—Alien Kid), Kelly Hoover (Mama Runt), Will Finn (Hollywood Fish), Dara McGarry (Hollywood Abby), Mark Kennedy (Hollywood Runt), Brad Abrell, Tom Amundsen, Steve Bencich, Greg Berg, Julianne Buescher, David Cowgill, Terri Douglas, Chris Edgerly, Amanda Fein, Caitlin Fein, Pat Fraley, Eddie Frierson, Jackie Gonneau, Archie Hahn, Jason Harris, Brittney Lee Harvey, Brian Herskowitz, Mandy Kaplan, Nathan Kress, Anne Lockhart, Connor Matheus, Mona Marshall, Scott Menville, Rene Mujica, Jonathan Nichols, Paul Pape, Aaron Spann, Pepper Sweeney, Scott Conrad, Ivan "Flipz" Velez

Synopsis

After Chicken Little causes mass hysteria when he mistakes a falling acorn for a piece of the sky, his name is mud in his hometown of Oakey Oaks. Down but not out, he struggles mightily to restore his reputation and make his dad, Buck Cluck, proud. Chicken Little joins the local baseball team and, despite the fact that he is barely bigger than a baseball himself, he manages to smack a championship-winning home run. With one crack of the bat, the town laughingstock becomes the toast of Oakey Oaks. Even Turkey Lurkey, the black-suited, spiffy mayor of the town (complete with stovepipe hat) is disappointed. But no sooner has Chicken Little redeemed himself than he is conked on the head one more time. And this time the sky really is falling! Fearful of once again being labeled crazy, Chicken Little tells no one but his best friends—Runt of the Litter; Abby Mallard, aka Ugly Duckling; and Fish Out of Water—about the threat that hangs over Oakey Oaks. Together this misfit crew tries to save the day. Chicken Little eventually discovers that he needs to risk his newfound popularity and alert his father and the town. When Buck realizes Chicken Little actually has it right this time, he unites with his son and his friends as they set out to save the world.

Sidelights

- In addition to his voice-over characterization of Mayor Turkey Lurkey, Don Knotts was originally cast as the narrator and recorded the lines with this intention. The producers decided to scrap that version and replaced him with producer/actor Garry Marshall, who handled the narration instead. A sample of the original Knotts opening narration can be found in the bonus materials of the film's DVD release.
- According to Walt Disney press materials for *Chicken Little:* "Walt Disney Feature Animation adds a whole new dimension to its legacy for memorable characters, great storytelling, and technical innovation with *Chicken Little,* the studio's first fully computer-animated feature film. A pioneer in using computers in animation since the early 1980s, Disney brings its distinct filmmaking style and approach to this exciting medium, along with a host of technical innovations. The result is a film that captures the very best qualities of Disney animation with a look and feel that audiences have never seen before. Adding to the excitement, *Chicken Little* is being presented in select theatres across the country in Disney Digital 3D™, a revolutionary new true three-dimensional digital experience. Disney teamed with effects powerhouse Industrial Light & Magic (ILM) to render the movie in 3D, and the film will be shown using specially installed Dolby® Digital Cinema systems."
- With the release of *Chicken Little,* Disney's first fully computer-animated feature is added to a historic, lengthy list of technical achievements created at the studio—including the first full-length animated feature film, *Snow White and the Seven Dwarfs,* in 1937.

Reviews

People: "Thanks to this splashy computer-animated debut, Disney has finally rediscovered its magical mojo. . . . Plenty of hilarious throwaway gags camouflage the thin storyline, which just barely sustains a feature length movie. Still, the result is easily Disney's most entertaining film since 1999's *Tarzan*. Once again, it seems the sky's the limit."

AIR BUDDIES

Released: 2006
Produced by: Anna McRoberts, Robert Vince
Written by: Anna McRoberts, Robert Vince
Directed by: Robert Vince
Running Time: 80 minutes
Walt Disney Home Entertainment

Cast

Slade Pearce (Noah), Trevor Wright (Grim), Abigail Breslin (Rosebud), Christian Pikes (Henry), Dominic Scott Kay (Bud-dha), Paul Rae (Denning), Michael Clarke Duncan (The Wolf), Don Knotts (Sniffer), Jarris Dashkewytch (Sam), Casey Beddow (Concession Attendant), Patrick Cranshaw (Sheriff Bob), Josh Flitter (Budderball), Tyler Foden (Bartleby Livingston), Spencer Fox (Mudbud), Skyler Gisondo (B-Dawg), Dan Joffre (Bob Framm), Irene Karas (Housekeeper), Richard Karn (Patrick Framm), Gig Morton (B-Dawg Boy), Holmes Osborne, Debra Jo Rupp (Voice of Pig), Tom Everett Scott (Buddy), Molly Shannon (Molly), Wallace Shawn (Voice of Goat), Jake D. Smith (Noah Framm—Archive Footage), Cynthia Stevenson (Jackie Framm), Mark Tisdale (Biker #2), Cainan Wiebe (Mud Bud Kid)

Synopsis

A continuation of the *Air Bud* films, *Air Buddies* has five adorable golden retriever puppies who venture off in a rescue mission to save their parents from evil dog-nappers. The puppies—called Rosebud, B-Dawg, Budderball, Mudbud, and Buddha—are in an adventure that involves using teamwork and learning the true meaning of family. The secret of the puppies that you will discover is that they can "talk"!

Sidelights

• This was Don Knotts's final film role, albeit a voice-over.

- The film's town of Fernfield is modeled after Mayberry, so it was a no-brainer for Don Knotts to voice the Deputy Sniffer.
- Robert Vince (producer/writer/director) recalled: "Of course Don is a legend, I remember him from *The Apple Dumpling Gang* and many, many other Disney movies, and he's always been somebody I've admired and wanted to work with. From a comedic perspective, I still consider him to be the best comedian ever, hands down. It will be the height of my career that I was able to work with Don."

Index

T

DON KNOTTS 1924-2006

About the Authors

STEPHEN COX, 42, is the author of more than twenty books on popular culture, film, and television, including *Here's Johnny!, One Fine Stooge, The Addams Chronicles, It's a Wonderful Life: A Memory Book, The Munsters,* and *The Munchkins of Oz.* He has written for the *Los Angeles Times, TV Guide,* and *SMOKE* magazine. In 1988, he graduated with honors from Park University in Kansas City, Missouri, with a BA in journalism and communication arts. Steve is a member of the Author's Guild and resides in Los Angeles.

KEVIN MARHANKA, 39, has been a collector of vintage film and television since he was a kid growing up in the Midwest. He has contributed to several books on popular culture (*Dreaming of Jeannie, Here on Gilligan's Isle, The Encyclopedia of TV Pets, Granny's Beverly Hillbillies Cookbook*). He has been a proud firefighter for eleven years in the Riverview Fire Protection District. He enjoys collecting autographs, a good German beer, and a fine cigar; he maintains an extensive collection on the musical group the Monkees. Kevin is the father of two daughters and resides in St. Louis.